Praise for
100 SOA Questions: Asked and Answered

"In this book, Kerrie and Ali truly capture the essence of SOA and its benefits to your Business and IT Deployments. Businesses today are desperate to be more nimble and innovative while reducing costs—a tricky proposition. SOA enables companies to reach these goals by tightly aligning the business and IT around the business processes, breaking those processes into reusable business and IT services, and allowing the underlying business and IT infrastructure to be more nimble in supporting the business goals. Effective SOA deployments also lay the groundwork for Cloud formations that can deliver even greater flexibility and cost saving to the business. This book clearly shows that a visit to the land of SOA and Cloud should be on every CxO's bucket list for their own business."

—**Daniel A. Powers**, VP Amazon Web Services Sales

"*100 SOA Questions* is a must-read for business and IT users who are interested in improving business innovation and agility. Based on their real-world experiences from hundreds of global customer engagements, Kerrie Holley and Ali Arsanjani do an outstanding job of explaining the multiple facets of SOA and providing a prescriptive approach to help readers incrementally unlock value from rigid business processes and antiquated application silos."

—**Manoj Saxena**, IBM Executive and Tech Entrepreneur

"In order for IT systems to be successful in today's world, they must be correct, complete, and extensible. For a long time we have had systems that are point-in-time complete, partially correct, and minimally extensible. Kerrie and Ali get to the heart of the matter when they speak to us about the DNA of a Service-Oriented Architecture. It has been my experience in working with them that their focus in defining granularity, composability, and loose coupling from the viewpoint and with the help of the business stakeholders is much more than the cliché, 'aligning IT with the business,' would lead you to believe."

—**Manny Bonet**, Software Architect

"It is the underpinning infrastructure of a system that determines ultimate flexibility and the ability to scale change to keep pace with rapidly changing global markets. Through Kerrie and Ali's simple, clear, and comprehensive articulation of the Service-Oriented Architecture approach, I can see that systems must pass through the maturing that SOA brings in order to leverage design methodologies of the future. Those who don't will be destined to revisit SOA. Great work, gentlemen, in showing us, in such a real world way, the differentiator needed to fight the fight in an ever-leveling technology playing field."

—**Robert Mansell**, Vice President,
Payments & Settlement Systems, PayPal

100 SOA Questions

100 SOA Questions

Asked and Answered

KERRIE HOLLEY
DR. ALI ARSANJANI

PRENTICE
HALL

Upper Saddle River, NJ • Boston • Indianapolis • San Francisco
New York • Toronto • Montreal • London • Munich • Paris • Madrid
Cape Town • Sydney • Tokyo • Singapore • Mexico City

Associate Publisher: Greg Wiegand
Senior Acquisitions Editor: Katherine Bull
Development Editor: Ginny Bess Munroe
Managing Editor: Kristy Hart
Senior Project Editor: Lori Lyons
Copy Editor: Keith Cline
Senior Indexer: Cheryl Lenser
Proofreader: Sheri Cain
Technical Reviewers: Chris Venable, Robert G. Laird
Publishing Coordinator: Cindy Teeters
Cover Designer: Alan Clements
Compositor: Nonie Ratcliff
Graphics: Laura Robbins

The publisher offers excellent discounts on this book when ordered in quantity for bulk purchases or special sales, which may include electronic versions and/or custom covers and content particular to your business, training goals, marketing focus, and branding interests. For more information, please contact:

U.S. Corporate and Government Sales
(800) 382-3419
corpsales@pearsontechgroup.com

For sales outside the United States, please contact:

International Sales
international@pearson.com

Visit us on the Web: informit.com/ph

Library of Congress Cataloging-in-Publication Data is on file.

ISBN-13: 978-0-137-08020-5
ISBN-10: 0-137-08020-4
Text printed in the United States on recycled paper at R.R. Donnelley, Crawfordsville, Indiana.
First printing November 2010

I dedicate this, my first book to:

*My wife, Gretchen McDougall, for her wisdom, love, beauty, support
and for blazing a trail of confidence to make this possible.*

*My oldest son, Kier Holley, for his maturity, kindness, intellect,
kindred spirit and paving a road that
always reminds me that the future is bright*

*My youngest son, Hugo Holley, for his old soul spirit,
sweet soul, who torched the road ahead and made it bright
by simply saying "Dad, just write it"*

*My brother, Laurence Holley, and my sister, Lynette Holley, whose
love and support has always created a steady path in my life*

*My mentor and second mother, Sue Duncan, founder of the Susan
Duncan Children's Center, for creating a world I could live in as a
child, and making the road I travel today possible*

—Kerrie Holley

I dedicate my first book to:

*My Grandparents, for showing me the Way with their
self-less devotion and unbending righteousness
to do well and achieve higher*

*My Mother, who has always been my Example to strive to achieve
more and yet take time to enjoy not only the academic
but also the beauty in life*

*My Wife, Parastoo, for her support and guidance,
for sense of duty and philanthropy*

My Son, Sam, for his passion and motivation, his spark and focus

*An unbounded ocean of love wakes up to itself
and finds these waves within.*

—Ali Arsanjani

Contents at a Glance

Contents

Preface

Almost two decades ago, I completed a project to develop and deploy a teller and sales application for a large U.S. bank. Enhanced business capabilities, technology upgrades in the branches, and a pending bank merger were the business drivers. Some months after the production roll-out, as the Chief Architect, I was invited to a meeting with the Vice Chairman of the Retail Banking who wanted to understand my perspective on how the bank should address challenges in meeting future demands that required extending the reach of the teller and sales platform functionality to other parts of the bank.

The Vice Chairman was responsible for all retail functions of the bank and expansion was hot on the agenda. The bank was growing, entering new market places, acquiring banks, opening branches, and rapidly attracting new customers. We sat down and discussed cross selling, expansion goals, and the need for several parts of the Bank such as credit card processing, wholesale banking, and loans, to be able to access and use functionality contained in the teller application we had just built and deployed. Obtaining customer information, account balance inquiries, and address updates were just a few of the basic pieces of functionality needed by these other departments but there were more complex pieces of business functionality required, too.

When wholesale banking or credit card processing needed to access data or functionality in the teller system, they needed to go through a development cycle that necessitated waiting in a queue with others, whereby the IT department could prioritize and satisfy the multiple requests and requirements. The Vice Chairman expressed this current situation as a problem; it impacted the bank's capability to get more products out the door faster and his ability to meet sales and revenue targets. He asked two questions: How can we do this better and how can the bank provide access to previously built and deployed business functionalities to other parts of the bank without going through IT development queues? Addressing this question and others by senior business executives has been top of mind for me for two decades.

Over the last decade, I have met with corporate executives from hundreds of companies across the world whose enterprises are characterized by disparate and siloed systems and applications; horizontal integration is the goal as businesses seek greater agility in the global marketplace. Corporate managers are asking how do to make the IT system more flexible so that it is easy to connect across the enterprise and so it is inexpensive in both time and cost. The story of the bank occurred two decades ago, but I find CEOs and other corporate executives asking this same question over and over again, decades later. Everyone is searching for flexibility as competition intensifies. Everyone sees this albatross around their neck getting uglier and negatively impacting goals for growth and limiting the responsiveness and agility required as the cost of maintaining, integrating, and supporting systems is rising. Less capital is available for innovation, changing the business, and delivering new capabilities.

Just a few years ago, I met with a corporate manager responsible for a payments business. His frustration was apparent as we discussed the need to change his three-year-old IT system to accommodate new channels (phones, kiosks, and other mobile devices) and new market segmentations. He was frustrated because although he was not a technologist or software engineer he knew something was not right. He wanted to know why after millions of dollars of investment in a creating a new payment system, built three years earlier, it was not easy to change his payment system to accommodate small and medium businesses or to allow access to payments using handheld devices.. He asked this question because his payment system was built with modern software engineering best practices yet flexibility was evasive: adding new channels and new customer segments would take too long and cost too much money as if he were building the system from scratch versus just changing the system. I responded and the short answer is that applying best practices and modern system engineering practices is not sufficient if agility is the goal. I further stated that there is a considerable amount of data that shows this problem is not isolated that most applications become difficult to change within 3 to 5 years after the first production deployment.

Recently, I was in Mexico City working with a large logistics company. It was just finishing an 18-month project to reengineer a core IT system that was no longer responsive to the business. The new system was engineered like the bank system two decades earlier, with the best software engineering practices and tools available. I was asked if this new system would suffer the fate of past systems in its capability to be responsive. That is, would this system become brittle in the future and if so, why? Would this new system be built for change such that flexibility was an attribute of the system and not a platitude? Again I answered no, stating that applying best practices alone will not achieve the goal of agility. I know this is true because his team and teams just like his around the world have been using modern and best practices of software engineering for years with the same results. The result is that three to five years after the system has been deployed it is difficult to change, and is expensive in time and money.

It is not only the commercial world that sees a problem but the public sector. we have met with various public sector organizations over the years and my interactions confirm that they are confronted with the same challenges we see in the private sector. :Public and private sector managers see the rising cost of support, integration, and maintenance of the systems as a ball and chain that is a huge drag on cost reduction and as a result, it puts a limit on monies available for creating new capabilities in the theater as the available dollars are limited.

It is these questions and their answers that prompted us to write this book about service-oriented architecture (SOA). This is not a technology book, but a book for technologists and business stakeholders. We hope to demonstrate, that SOA and service-orientation in general, is not solely a technology play but a paradigm and architecture that calls for business and IT collaboration and when understood and applied, it can change the course of your business, where flexibility and lower total cost of ownership become realities.

Total cost of ownership and flexibility are different sides of the same coin. There is less flexibility when funds are not available to spend or when providing new capabilities is constrained because resources are consumed in integration, maintenance, and support.

Flexibility is evident when the business, not IT, has the power to deploy new business features without IT development queues or when new capabilities can be provided in weeks or months instead of years, and when two or more capabilities can be composed at will to create a new, enhanced capability that directly supports business drivers and alleviates painpoints.

> If we make the right choices, we will have a chance to escape from the boxes that frustrate us today. The escape will not be easy —we will be constantly challenged to question conventional assumptions and comfortable practices. Many will not even see the opportunity. They will continue to remain closed in the boxes that make every day more frustrating. Some will see the opportunity but will either try to move too quickly or fail to stay the course. They will blame the technology for its failure to produce results. For those few who succeed, the rewards will make the journey well worth the effort.
>
> —John Hagel III in *Out of the Box*

Our choice as managers, leaders, or architects is to seize the opportunity and release ourselves from self-imposed boxed thinking because "if you don't change anything, nothing changes." We can make business flexibility a reality with IT support but it requires a vision, a strategy, execution of the strategy, and most importantly, staying the course. The strategy must be a living plan accompanied with a evolving roadmap that can be implemented, monitored, and measured. It requires you take incremental steps that together bring about change: incremental and quantum leaps over time.

If you want to get out of the boxes that John describes, enabling your IT systems to be engines of innovation, this book will be of value. If you are responsible for strategy in the organization and need to link that strategy to an IT strategy to make your IT systems and infrastructure capable of supporting a rapidly changing landscape or business model, you should read this book. If you are tired of reading about platitudes and seek guidance about how to achieve business flexibility through the adoption of SOA, you will obtain value in reading this book. This book is not about a technology change; it's about a business journey with IT, where SOA is both the enabler and the catalyst.

This book is different than other books on SOA as content is organized into 100 questions and answers. Feel free to go directly to the chapter that most interests you or go directly to a question for which you would like an answer. Visit www.100Questions.info and submit any questions that remain unanswered.

Kerrie Holley

Acknowledgments

We want to thank the countless number of colleagues and clients who have helped shape our thinking. The problems they've presented and perspectives they've shared have helped us acquire valuable knowledge.

Although the list is long, we do want to acknowledge specific individuals whose insights and experience have allowed us to learn so much. Thank you to Sarah Garrison, Doug Hunt, and Robert LeBlanc, who got us started on our SOA journey. A thank you to George Galambos and Raghu Varadan, who taught us so much. Thank you to Ray Harishankar, Liang-Jie Zhang, Kishore Channabasavaiah, Shankar Kalyana, Rob High, Rolando Franco, William A. Brown, Abdul Allam, Chris Venable, Siddharth N. Purohit, Brian Paulsen, Jenny Ang, Julian Petriuc, Claudio Cozzi, Richard Disney, Mamdouh Ibrahim, Olaf Zimmermann, Robert Laird, Arun Thakore, Tony Cowan, Rick Robinson, David Janson, Raphael P. Chancey, Manish Vipani, Manoj Saxena, Isabel Van Mele, Ko-Yang Wang, Marc Fiammante, Denise Hatzidakis, Alexei Chirokikh, Don Ferguson, Pamela K. Isom, Manny Bonet, Waseem Roshen, Chuck Gupta, Rachel Reintz, Boris Veroeveren, Jose Loya, Geert-Willem Haasjes, Luba Cherbakov, Ian Turton, and Shuvanker Ghosh, all of whom contributed immensely to our knowledge base.

This book would not be possible without the people at Pearson Education. We thank Ginny Bess Munroe for her encouragement and superb skills as the development editor. Thanks also to the rest of the Production team. Robert Laird and Chris Venable did a remarkable job of reviewing our manuscript and provided valuable insight as to which questions really mattered.

This book would not be possible without the support, patience, project management skills, guidance, perseverance, and leadership of our editor, Katherine Bull. Katherine worked to cultivate the idea for this book, labored to sell the idea, and encouraged us as writers. Katherine showed a tremendous amount of patience, provided endless hours of support, and without her confidence and project management, this book would never have come together.

About the Authors

Kerrie Holley has a wealth of experience in application development, software engineering, systems engineering, IT consulting, and enterprise architecture. Mr. Holley has operated as Chief Architect, Strategist, Consultant, and Designer on more than fifty SOA projects. In his current role, he oversees hundreds of SOA projects in their technical direction, strategy, and successful deployment. Mr. Holley's current focus is on the convergence of business rules, business process management, analytics, and SOA in making businesses more agile. Mr. Holley holds several SOA patents and has a BA in mathematics from DePaul University and a Juris Doctorate degree from DePaul School of Law. Mr. Holley has worked in a senior capacity for several companies, including Bank of America, Tandem Computers, Ernst & Young and is currently an IBM Fellow.

Dr. Arsanjani is a rare mix of industry hands-on consulting and academic research that he leverages in his Chief Technology Officer role as advisor to high-profile companies. Through his experience as strategist, consultant, and architect, he has helped companies achieve business performance through leveraging and changing IT. His current area of focus is to enable companies to achieve higher levels of business performance and enable them to optimize their business through the agility gained in concert with IT and business operations. Ali Arsanjani has chaired standard bodies such as The Open Group and is responsible for co-leading the SOA Reference Architecture, SOA Maturity Model, and Cloud Computing Architecture standards. In his role as Chief Architect, he and his team specialize in harvesting and developing best-practices for the modeling, analysis, design, and implementation of SOA and Web Services on hundreds of projects.

He is a hands-on, sought-after architect around the world on large SOA projects, and he is the principal author of the industry first Service-Oriented Modeling and Architecture (SOMA) method for SOA. His work on variation-oriented analysis allows companies to build less software but achieve higher gains, and his patterns for service-oriented software architecture combine SOA with business process management, business rules, and analytics to achieve higher levels of maturity for organizations.

Introduction

You will never stub your toe standing still. The faster you go, the more chance there is of stubbing your toe, but the more chance you have of getting somewhere.
—Charles Kettering

A myth abounds that ostriches hide their head in the sand when frightened, and that same behavior is often attributed to anyone who foolishly ignores problems while hoping those problems magically vanish. The ostrich does many things, but hiding its head in the sand is not one of them. IT departments do many things, and hiding their heads in the sand is unfortunately one of them.

IT departments face many challenges, one of the biggest being that they spend a substantial part of their resources on running the business rather than changing the business. That is, they spend substantially more money on maintenance than on innovation. And this particular problem is getting worse and cannot be improved upon by inertia or standing still. Instead, change is required, and this book covers how to adopt *service-oriented architecture* (SOA) as a change agent (and deal with the inevitable stubbed toes along the way).

Several forces and events contribute to inefficiencies and higher costs for many IT departments: acquisitions, fiefdoms, technology zealots, infrastructures built over time without a roadmap, financial measurements that incent IT to be cheaper rather than more effective, poor application portfolio management, and ineffective architectural policies. The effects of such inhibit IT departments' ability to accelerate or improve time to market for new business capabilities. SOA can make a significant and positive difference, but you must understand that this is a process, a true journey. After all, technology implementation by itself does not guarantee business agility.

About This Book

According to your needs and familiarity with SOA, you can use this book as a textbook, quick reference guide, or a tutorial. You do not need to read the book sequentially. In fact, you can start at any chapter and even jump between chapters to learn about the areas that interest you, and you can do so without losing context/continuity.

This book inventories challenging questions from business and IT stakeholders and provides corresponding answers. Where appropriate, the answers are prescriptive. Although, in this book, we attempt to exhaustively anticipate your questions and provide readily understandable answers, we also prove an outside forum for you to ask, in your own words, any questions we might have failed to address. You can access this forum at www.100Questions.info. We invite you to continue our SOA dialogue there.

Questions are numbered sequentially from 1 to 100 throughout the entire book.

Intended Audience

This book is intended for executives, managers, IT architects, business architects, business analysts, line-of-business (LOB) managers, and students who want to understand the basic and complex concepts of SOA and the business and technology rationales for developing and implementing SOA.

For example, readers might include the following:

- LOB/product managers who wonder what SOA has to do with the business
- Business executives/stakeholders who want to know how to make new development projects have built-in flexibility and sustained agility
- Business/IT stakeholders who want to know what they need to do differently to make systems more agile

- Architects tasked with a transformation initiative or project and who want to understand how or whether SOA can be applied
- Architects who want to understand how to build a system for change so that the application is not difficult to change three or five years after its initial production deployment
- Enterprise architects who want to be more effective at creating adaptive and usable enterprise architectures
- Students and others who want to know the facts about SOA

How This Book Is Organized

This book is organized in such a way that you can browse and easily find topics of interest. The chapters themselves address specific domains of concern about SOA in the business/IT world, as follows:

Chapter 1, "SOA Basics"—This chapter defines *SOA* and *service orientation.* It also examines several myths and misconceptions that prevail in the marketplace about SOA.

Chapter 2, "Business"—This chapter examines the forces that drive businesses in all industries to become more agile, adaptable, responsive, resilient, and profitable. The chapter covers how to address the business value of SOA, sell SOA to business stakeholders, and the return on investment of SOA. This chapter also covers *business process management* (BPM).

Chapter 3, "Organization"—This chapter discusses the technology and organizational roadblocks that impede forward motion in SOA adoption. The chapter also examines the relationships between business and IT and how they collaborate for SOA.

Chapter 4, "Governance"—This chapter addresses the hot topic of governance, including why it is important and its impact on achieving business results with SOA adoption. The chapter answers questions about governance, adoption steps, how to get started, and how to communicate the SOA journey.

Chapter 5, "Methods"—This chapter addresses questions on methods, both business and system. Service granularity and identification of services are also covered in this chapter.

Chapter 6, "Applications"—This chapter distinguishes between applications and composite applications and identifies what changes about applications as a result of SOA.

Chapter 7, "Architecture"—This chapter considers architecture from various views (for example, application architecture, integration architecture, and enterprise architecture) and discusses the impact the various views and their interrelationships with SOA.

Chapter 8, "Information"—This chapter covers how information, data architecture, and management support SOA. Concepts addressed in this chapter include information as a service, canonical models, and message models.

Chapter 9, "Infrastructure"—This chapter covers the middleware and operating environment required for SOA. Topics addressed include the enterprise service bus, registries, operational impacts of SOA, and the required operational maturity of the infrastructure to support SOA.

Chapter 10, "Future"—The last chapter of this book deals with the future of SOA. Where is it and where is it going? Is SOA dead? Isn't cloud computing the replacement and our next horizon? What is meant by context-aware services?

At the end of each chapter, we address common pitfalls and how to avoid them. After all, before organizations can take preemptive measures to avoid missteps in SOA adoptions and initiatives, they must understand where others are making mistakes.

1

SOA Basics

Delusions, errors, and lies are like huge, gaudy vessels, the rafters of which are rotten and worm-eaten, and those who embark in them are fated to be shipwrecked.
—Buddha

Service-oriented architecture (SOA) is defined in a number of ways, but not all definitions are equal, and not all definitions are complete. Instead of just providing another definition of SOA, this chapter describes the basic building blocks of SOA and looks at the value proposition of SOA from key stakeholder perspectives. Besides covering the basic building blocks of SOA, its DNA, and the value propositions of adopting SOA and its ultimate utility, this chapter describes what makes an implementation an SOA deployment. Specifically, this chapter addresses the following questions:

1. What is SOA?
2. Is SOA an architectural style?
3. What are fundamental constructs (the DNA) of SOA?
4. What is the difference between a Web Service and an SOA service?
5. What makes a project an SOA implementation?

SOA Basics: Q&A

1. What Is SOA?

Numerous vendors, application providers, system integrators, architects, authors, analysts firms, and standards bodies provide definitions of SOA. The definitions of SOA are diverse. Most are complementary and do not conflict with each other. SOA has a variety of definitions because the definition is often tuned to a specific audience, as explaining SOA to a CEO is different from explaining SOA to a programmer. The term *service orientation* is often used synonymously with SOA, but just like SOA it has a wide range of interpretations. Service orientation is broader and represents a way of thinking about services in the context of business and IT. This book makes no distinction between SOA and service orientation and in some cases may use the two terms synonymously.

An agreed-upon definition for SOA eludes the industry. Anyone reading Wikipedia's definition page for SOA will see the challenges of trying to gain consensus on an SOA definition. Standards bodies, the OASIS group, and the Open Group have provided complementary but different SOA definitions. Presented with a blank sheet of paper, an artist sees a canvas. A poet might fill it with verse. An engineer seizes the opportunity to make a paper plane. Kids may see it as a future pile of spit wads. SOA is that blank sheet of paper.

To the *chief information officer* (CIO), SOA is a journey that promises to reduce the lifetime cost of the application portfolio, maximize *return on investment* (ROI) in both application and technology resources, and reduce lead times in delivering solutions to the business.

To the business executive, SOA is a set of services that can be exposed to their customers, partners, and other parts of the organization. Business capabilities, function, and business logic can be combined and recombined to serve the needs of the business now and tomorrow. Applications serve the business because they are composed of services that can be quickly modified or redeployed in new business contexts, allowing the business to quickly respond to changing customer needs, business opportunities, and market conditions.

To the business analyst, SOA is a way of unlocking value, because business processes are no longer locked in application silos. Applications no longer operate as inhibitors to changing business needs.

To the chief architect or enterprise architect, SOA is a means to create dynamic, highly configurable and collaborative applications built for change. SOA reduces IT complexity and rigidity. SOA becomes the solution to stop the gradual entropy that makes applications brittle and difficult to change. SOA reduces lead times and costs because reduced complexity makes modifying and testing applications easier when they are structured using services.

To the IT architect, SOA is the architectural solution for integrating diverse systems by providing an architectural style that promotes loose coupling and reuse. Many IT architects think they have seen this style before with earlier architectural initiatives such as DCE, the *Distributed Computing Environment,* and CORBA, the *Common Object Request Broker Architecture.*

To the developer, SOA is a programming model or paradigm where web services and contracts becomes a dominant design for interoperability. It is a web service when it uses a *Web Service Description Language* (WSDL) or equivalent specification for describing the service. Web services enable organizations to communicate information, using messages, without intimate knowledge of each other's IT systems.

Delivering on the promises of SOA (improved business agility, maximized ROI, reduced IT complexity and rigidity, reduced costs, reduced lead times, reduced risk, new opportunities to deliver value, increased participation in value networks, and incremental implementation) requires you take a holistic view of SOA. If we limit the view of SOA to a single stakeholder (e.g., IT architect, developer, or business analyst) the benefits will not accrue because SOA then just becomes one in a long list of overhyped technologies rather than a novel approach to building flexible business solutions.

2. Is SOA an Architectural Style?

SOA is often seen as an architectural style that has been around for years. Figure 1.1 shows the architectural style of SOA. In this scenario, a service consumer invokes or uses a service. The service consumer uses the service description to obtain necessary information about the provider service (e.g., account service) to be consumed. The service description provides the binding information so the consumer can connect to the service, and the description identifies the various operations (e.g., open or close account) available from the provider service. A broker can be used to find the service using a registry that houses information about the service and its location.

In Figure 1.1, it is difficult to determine how the architecture style of SOA enables the strategic benefits of SOA, such as lowering the lifetime cost of an application or bringing faster time to market or making applications resilient to change. SOA as an architectural style often makes an SOA project solely an IT endeavor where the strategic business benefits of SOA no longer become the focus or measured outcomes. Benefits of process flexibility, time-to-market savings, lower costs, and others can be achieved with SOA, but only if we holistically adopt all stakeholder views of SOA and its application and pursue SOA adoption accordingly. When pundits, architects, consultants, or executives define SOA as a pure technology play or as solely an architectural style, they relegate it to the realm of IT science projects, overhyped technologies, and a marketing strategy *rather than a novel approach to building flexible business solutions.*

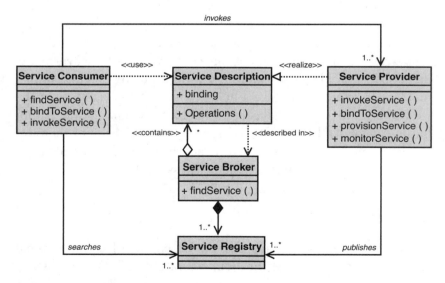

Figure 1.1   SOA as an architecture style

An understanding of SOA is enhanced with the next question and answer. By looking at the SOA building blocks of SOA, you can gain a fuller understanding of what SOA is and how to realize its promised benefits.

3. What Are the Fundamental Constructs (the DNA) of SOA?

The most basic construct or building block of SOA is a service. Software engineering over the years has evolved from procedural to structured programming to object-oriented programming to component-based development and now to service oriented. Figure 1.2 illustrates the different levels of abstraction from objects to services. Each evolution of abstraction builds on the previous, and SOA embraces the best practices of object and component development.

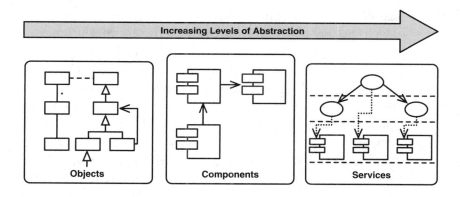

Figure 1.2   Levels of abstraction

To see architectural style of SOA, refer to Figure 1.1. That illustration shows the fundamental constructs of SOA, such as the service consumer and the service provider and their relationship. The consumer invokes a service, the business functionality, by contract. The provider of the service defines the contract as a service description. An intermediary, such as a broker, uses a registry to find or search for published services. Service consumer, service provider, service description, service broker, and a registry are all part of the DNA of SOA.

A service in SOA is the logical, self-contained business function. Services in SOA have the following attributes:

- **Stateless:** SOA services neither remember the last thing they were asked to do nor do they care what the next is. Services are not dependent on the context or state of other services, only on their functionality. Talking on the telephone is stateful, whereas posting a letter is stateless. The World Wide Web provides an excellent example, where each request from a user for a web page or URL results in the requested pages being served, but without the web server remembering the request later. Each request or communication is discrete and unrelated to requests that precede or follow it.

- **Discoverable:** A service must be discoverable by potential consumers of the service. After all, if a service is not known to exist, it is unlikely ever to be used. Services are published or exposed by service providers in the SOA service directory, from which they are discovered and invoked by service consumers.

- **Self-describing:** The SOA service interface describes, exposes, and provides an entry point to the service. The interface contains all the information a service consumer needs to discover and connect to the service, without ever requiring the consumer to understand (or even see) the technical implementation details.

- **Composable:** SOA services are, by nature, composite. They can be composed from other services and, in turn, can be combined with other services to compose new business solutions.

- **Loose coupling:** Loose coupling allows the concerns of application features to be separated into independent pieces. This separation of concern provides a mechanism for one service to call another without being tightly bound to it. Separation of concerns is achieved by establishing boundaries, where a boundary is any logical or physical separation that delineates a given set of responsibilities. For example, an account service has open account, authorization, and audit features representing delineations of responsibilities and three separations of concerns.

- **Governed by policy:** Services are built by contract. Relationships between services (and between services and service domains) are governed by policies and *service-level agreements* (SLAs), promoting process consistency and reducing complexity.

- **Independent location, language, and protocol:** Services are designed to be location transparent and protocol/platform independent (generally speaking, accessible by any authorized user, on any platform, from any location).

In addition, services in a service-oriented architecture typically have the following characteristics:

- **Coarse-grained:** Services are typically coarse-grained business functions. Granularity is a statement of functional richness for a service—the more coarse-grained a service is, the richer the function offered by the service. Coarse-grained services reduce complexity for system developers by limiting the steps necessary to fulfill a given business function, and they reduce strain on system resources by limiting the "chattiness" of the electronic conversation. Applications by nature are coarse-grained because they encompass a large set of functionality; the components that comprise applications would be fine-grained. Similarly, within an application, a service such as "get account information" (which returns name, account number, and address) could be described as coarse-grained, whereas a service to "get account number" could be described as fine- grained.

- **Asynchronous:** Asynchronous communication is not required of an SOA service, but it does increase system scalability through asynchronous behavior and messaging techniques. Unpredictable network latency and high communications costs can slow response times in an SOA environment, due to the distributed nature of services. Asynchronous behavior and messaging allow a service to issue a service request and then continue processing until the service provider returns a response.

Viewed from the top down, SOA comprises the following constructs, as illustrated in Figure 1.3: consumer, business processes, services, components, information, rules, and policies. Consumers allow invocation or composition of services at the consumer layer through social software, mashups, business processes, or other systems. Business processes represent the flows of activities required to complete a business process; they are compositions of services targeted to achieve business goals. Services are the main structuring element required by a service consumer and are provided by the service provider. Services offer functionality and quality of service,

both of which are externalized within service descriptions and policies. Services can be composed of other services, thus making them
composite services. Components realize not only the functionality of
the services they expose but also ensure their quality of service. Information flows between the layers (for example, consumer, process,
and service) and within a layer. Lastly, rules and policies exist for services, components, and flows.

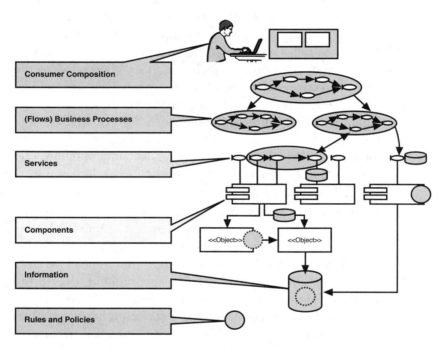

Figure 1.3   Top-down view of SOA constructs

Although objects are illustrated in Figure 1.3, the word *object*
does not imply an implementation of object orientation, because the
object can easily be a procedural subroutine implemented in a multi-
tude of languages as easily as it can be implemented in a object-
oriented programming language. SOA must have services and
components that realize the services. Processes or flows may string
services together to fulfill a step or activity of a business process. For
example a transfer of funds service may string together both a debit
and credit account service.

There is also a technology view of SOA. Technology enables SOA, makes it efficient, and optimizes the implementation, but SOA is not defined by the technologies chosen for implementation. Instead, SOA is defined by providing a uniform means to offer, discover, interact with, and use capabilities (services) to produce desired effects consistent with measurable expectations.

The major technologies associated with SOA include business-focused tools, software construction tools, and middleware technologies. Figure 1.4 illustrates the basic technology building blocks for SOA. Tools are required for SOA addressing design-time and run-time scenarios. Business stakeholders use business-focused tools for modeling and analysis of business processes and flows, and they will also use business activity monitoring technology to gain insights into business performance of processes and workflow. IT practitioners use a set of tools for development of business applications and for managing the operating environment addressing integration, monitoring, and security.

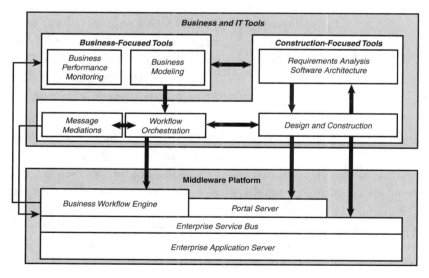

Figure 1.4   Business and IT tools for SOA

The DNA of SOA will most likely be further investigated and defined by standards groups actively involved in defining an SOA

ontology. For example, see www.opengroup.org/projects/soa-ontol-
ogy/. Such an ontology will address SOA key concepts, including services, service contracts, service interfaces, composition (orchestration,
choreography, and collaboration), processes, service compositions,
policies, and events. Each of these makes up the DNA of SOA.

4. What Is the Difference Between a Web Service and an SOA Service?

The distinction between business services or SOA services versus a
web service is not often articulated, and many equate the two as being
the same. SOA services can be realized as web services, but not all web
services are equal to SOA services. Web services represent the use of
both a published standard and a set of technologies for invocation and
interoperability. SOA services are services that fulfill a key step or activity of a business process and can be described as business services and
are often exposed as web services.

Figure 1.3 illustrates both an SOA service and a web service. The
picture shows the difference between SOA and web services at runtime (i.e., implementation level) and at design time. The web service
is illustrated on the right side of Figure 1.5, specifically the *Web Services Description Language* (WSDL) and its attributes such as port
types and operations. The attribute that makes it a web service is the
use of WSDL or equivalent.

In design, we identify and specify a service that provides the
design, or we identify and specify interfaces that include method
specifications. The combination of the definition of the method and
the interface at design time is what we refer to as a *service* from an
SOA perspective. Use cases can be used to capture the functional
requirements for a service. Figure 1.5 contrasts the differences
between a service in SOA and a web service. Both SOA services and
web services are part of the DNA of SOA.

In an SOA, business processes, activities, and workflow are broken down into constituent functional elements called services. They
can be accessed and used directly by applications, or they can be
mixed and matched with other services to create new business capabilities. Business services or SOA services are reusable business

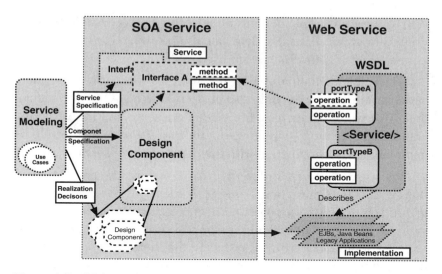

Figure 1.5   SOA service and web service

capabilities. Examples in banking include open account or change address. For transportation, it might be get reservation or hold reservation, and with loan processing, get loan, apply for loan, and update address are examples of business services. Business processes are also key constructs of SOA, part of its DNA.

5. What Makes a Project an SOA Implementation?

The deployment of services makes a project an SOA implementation, where a *service* is defined in the preceding answer as a web service or an SOA service. The use of the *Web Service Description Language* (WSDL) or equivalent makes a service a web service. An SOA service must satisfy the criteria described in the Answer 2; namely, an SOA service must be stateless; discoverable; self-describing; composable; loosely coupled; governed; and independent of location, language, or protocol. That is, the use of services alone makes the project or implementation an SOA implementation. However, an SOA implementation may not accrue the desired benefits of SOA around cost savings, reuse, time to market, or flexibility.

Services can have different levels of maturity. For example, services can be ad hoc in their design and implementation where a

WSDL façade is implemented to make function accessible to other systems or applications. Services can also be architected where service modeling and governance are used to maximize service reuse.

The implementation of SOA technologies without a deployment of one or more services could also be defined as an SOA implementation. This would be atypical because middleware and infrastructure implementations (e.g., a registry or enterprise service bus) would be implemented in conjunction with the deployment of services.

Just as services have different levels of maturity, so do SOA adoptions within an organization. Some SOA adoptions require a program of projects to address a journey of increasing maturity to achieve strategic SOA goals of building systems for change, infusing flexibility as an attribute of systems, or reducing the lifetime costs of applications and infrastructure. In this case, the program comprises a series of SOA projects that incrementally raise the maturity of SOA in an organization and along the way enable the realization of the strategic SOA benefits.

Often, because of overselling of SOA, organization leaders, managers, and executives wrongly believe that the benefits of SOA automatically accrue when an SOA implementation occurs. SOA has varied and diverse definitions, and hence its implementations are equally varied. So, organizations seeking to accrue any of the promised benefits of SOA must do more than focus on SOA implementations. That is, each expected benefit of SOA requires a different level of SOA maturity. For example, if the goal is only to reduce the cycle time of a business process that deals with external partners, exposing web services may be the only necessary SOA adoption. However, if the business goal is to reduce time to market for new products, this requires a broader adoption of SOA that addresses reusable services, structuring of applications using services, improving integration using services, and aspects of SOA governance to address service sharing, funding, and ownership.

SOA Basics: Key Concepts

This chapter's answers emphasized the utility of SOA and how to accrue its strategic and tactical benefits, instead of just providing an agreed-upon definition. However, looking at the definition through the lens of the different stakeholders provides a comprehensive view of what SOA is highlights the various potentials of SOA. The DNA of SOA comprises service consumers, business processes, services, service descriptions, components, information, rules, policies, web services, technologies (e.g., registries and brokers), and tools that address business and IT domains.

As you learned in this chapter, SOA implementations are as varied as SOA definitions, and the benefits that accrue depend on the maturity of SOA adoption within an organization. Organizations and executives who expect to accrue strategic benefits of SOA will need to treat SOA adoption as a journey realized incrementally by project (not as tactical goals, where a project might be sufficient). The next chapter answers questions that business leaders and executives ask about SOA.

2

Business

Competitive differentiation in the insurance industry is like a sailboat race; in a given boat race, all the competitors will be in the same design class, meaning everybody has the same type of boat, the same sails, and the same number of crew members. That being the case, if you're behind someone, you're going to be behind them until the finish line unless you try something different. Tactical errors of your opponents aside, to get ahead, you're going to have to take a different tack.

—Fred Matteson

It was with great interest that I read the article "IT Doesn't Matter" by Nicholas G. Carr in the *Harvard Business Review* in 2003. Of course, the article was less about whether IT mattered and more an assertion that the opportunity for strategic differentiation using IT has diminished. Carr acknowledges that IT has operational value for business, but argues that IT should be managed as a commodity, with the business focus in IT on cost optimization, continuous availability, and security (so as not to disrupt business operations). He writes that IT has become ordinary, as necessary as accounting departments and legal teams, but easily replicated and readily available; like its predecessors, the railroad, telegraph, and electricity, competitive differentiation using IT is a thing of the past.

Comparing IT to technology (e.g., the railroad, telegraph, electricity, or computer products) is like comparing music to instruments. Just as in music, differentiation and a competitive edge goes to those who create value. The music is not mere a by-product of instruments, and IT is not a by-product of technology. Some organizations use IT as a strategic force and lead the market, others choose to be fast followers, and others followers. Differentiation and value occurs as a result of several factors and not because everyone bought the same technology, the same instruments. Just as in the sailboat race, competitors can buy the same sailboat and hire similar crews, but only one winner emerges. In business, everyone can buy the same technology, but it's what an organization does differently, the application of technology, that makes a difference.

The degree to which IT matters in areas of strategic advantage and differentiation will vary by business based on its market, size, and business model. For a small three-person company or a 100-person company, having a personal computer, email, word processing, and spreadsheet software suffice (because IT is a commodity to many small companies). For companies trying to beat the competition, seeking innovation to increase market share, seeking differentiation to increase revenue and profits, where world-class responsiveness and agility matters, *IT matters*.

Responsiveness and effectiveness require a strategy and successful implementation of the strategy. The enterprise, company, or line of business that does not have a strategy is like a machine that coasts downhill at the mercy of any bump in the road. The company that does not implement its strategies is a stalled machine slowly rusting. Service-oriented architecture (SOA) should be a part of any IT strategy because it provides approaches and architecture for making a business more responsive. This chapter continues question numbering from Chapter 1. This chapter is focused on the business value of SOA and how the business can implement its strategy with SOA as a key implementation approach by addressing the following questions:

6. Why should business stakeholders care about SOA?

7. How should SOA be sold to the business or business stakeholder?

8. What is the return on investment (ROI) of SOA adoption?

9. How should the business measure the effectiveness of SOA?

10. What are the criteria for selecting a project for SOA adoption?

11. What is flexibility and how does SOA deliver on this promise?

12. How is reuse accomplished using SOA?

13. What should business or business stakeholders do differently because of SOA?

14. Can SOA be applied to business architecture or should it be used solely for IT?

15. What are the common pitfalls from a business vantage point in adopting SOA?

Business: Q&A

6. Why Should Business Stakeholders Care About SOA?

Companies that need customizable solutions or use IT for competitive value, companies seeking to leverage IT capabilities for business advantage, these are companies that should care about SOA. Business stakeholders should care about SOA adoption if a business wants to be more responsive to their markets, increase market share, and improve customer loyalty, anything that represents a business outcome where IT can make a difference. Many of these benefits cannot be realized without a synergistic relationship between business and IT, which requires that stakeholders in business and IT understand enough about SOA to help make its promised benefits a reality. Although IT has a larger role in SOA adoption, active business participation will be necessary to achieve strategic goals and ensuing SOA benefits. The strategic goals SOA makes possible and how business and IT collaborate to make these goals come to life are explored in this and subsequent chapters.

Figure 2.1 illustrates the challenges many companies face when using IT to make a difference and the business benefits provided with SOA adoption. Integration costs represents one of the largest expenses in enhancing and maintaining systems, a cost that can be minimized and avoided in many cases. IT may take too long to respond to changing business requirements for a variety of reasons. Chapter 5, "Methods," and Chapter 6, "Applications," explain how SOA can accelerate delivery for IT and help IT become more efficient and more responsive. Existing and legacy systems constrain many organizations because they must perform workarounds, invest heavily in a new system or rewriting of an existing system, or worse, lower their aspirations as they seek to configure or change business processes based on new market demands and opportunities. Getting the required ROI on software/hardware upgrades is increasingly challenging.

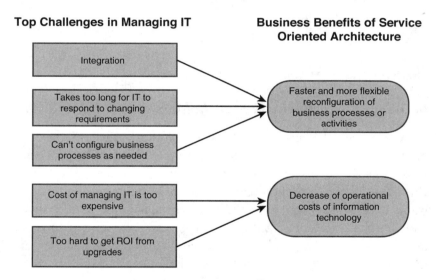

Figure 2.1   Business benefits of SOA

The rising cost of managing IT (that is, running the business) is a significant issue, as illustrated in Figure 2.2. As this figure shows, the average company spends as much as 85% of its IT budget to keep existing operations and only 15% of its budget on changing the business, innovation, or new capabilities for the business. The optimum IT budget split focuses on efficiency and innovation, not spending. Companies who find themselves close to spending the 85% on operations, integration, and keeping the lights on risk completely losing their IT-driven business agility. Companies that care about SOA are those companies that know it's a necessity to spend on IT to create capabilities that innovate, differentiate, and change the business in a way that creates desired business outcomes. SOA is the preferred architectural approach, a blueprint for making both the business and IT more efficient such that a company can spend 40% of its IT budget on creating new business capabilities. Many organizations are not seizing the moment as their SOA initiatives are stalled (or worse, failed), and in every instance where this is true, the common pattern is that SOA is solely IT driven, with minimal if any business collaboration. IT solutions in the long term will cost the business more in spending and a lot more in lost opportunity (e.g., flexibility), and for these two reasons, business stakeholders should care about SOA.

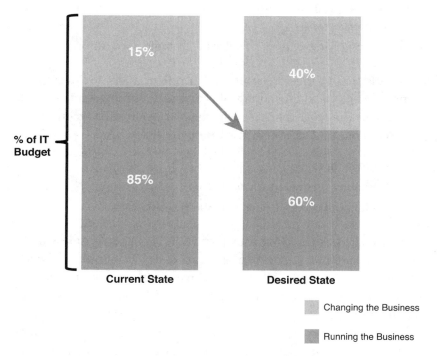

Figure 2.2   An optimum IT budget focuses on innovation.

One fact is clear to organizations that leverage IT for competitive value: Business pressures are mounting as IT constraints are rising. By adopting an SOA, organizations can remove many IT constraints and thus create new opportunities for business to become faster, more responsive, and more flexible. The most valuable attribute that an organization can have is flexibility: flexibility to meet market demands, customer needs, and flexibility to exploit opportunities before they are lost. If any of the following are true about an organization, it's a reason for business to care about SOA and pursue SOA adoption:

- Pursuing business or IT transformation initiatives
- Seeking faster time to value from IT
- Transforming or modernizing strategic applications
- Attempting to lower the lifetime cost of applications or infrastructure
- Pursuing reuse as a goal to bring products or capabilities to the market faster
- Looking for greater flexibility in strategic applications

In addition to these reasons, which reflect a journey (a strategic purpose) where it will take multiple years and a series of initiatives to bring about the goal, there are also less-strategic, more-tactical reasons to pursue SOA adoption, including the following:

- Increasing revenue
- Reducing business process cycles
- Reducing time and costs for systems integration

Organizations pursuing transformation activities, business or IT, embark on similar strategic planning processes: They gather business goals and requirements, conduct gap analysis to compare the current situation to the future, research options, and develop a strategy to be implemented. These strategic processes are iterative, collaborative, and when effective, continuous. The current state for most include an IT investment plan based on departmental and functional requests leading to less-optimized IT spending; inflexible architectures; rising IT total spend so that less monies are available for innovation and new solutions; practices, methods, and technologies based on individual projects versus strategic goals; silo approaches; and lack of a unified or integrated view of their customers. SOA adoption provides an architectural approach for implementing aspects of both business and IT transformations. In fact, when developing a strategy, most if not all organizations research options and recognize the need to embrace SOA as the preferred architectural approach. SOA becomes a key element of the strategy. Of course strategies are ineffective without successful execution and outcomes are brought about when SOA adoption is successful.

Seeking faster time to value from IT, transforming or modernizing strategic assets (applications), lowering the lifetime cost of applications, reusing the business functions often locked in applications, and greater flexibility in strategic applications—these are all reasons for business stakeholders to both understand SOA and collaborate with IT on adoption. Each of these represents strategic concerns requiring business and IT collaboration. SOA adoption for tactical, short-term concerns is another reason to care about SOA. This often entails exposing existing business functions to third parties for new revenue opportunities or exposing services to streamline and make more efficient a process used by external partners. For example, telecommunication companies are exposing the legacy capability of a mobile device's location as a location service allowing a wide range of mobile applications to invoke the service to locate lost phones, track their children whereabouts or meet friends for dinner who happen to be nearby.

7. How Should SOA Be Sold to the Business or Business Stakeholder?

If possible, IT stakeholders should avoid selling SOA to the business and instead should focus on specific strategic and tactical business and IT concerns. Instead of focusing on SOA, organizations should ask themselves what problem they are trying to solve. Figure 2.3 shows the basic reasons for SOA adoption. If any of these concerns is present, a business scenario should be drafted for each concern, as many as possible, and these scenarios addressing specific pain points should serve as the basis for change. For example, if the business goal is to move to architectures capable of business agility and game-changing business models, a business scenario should describe something the business cannot do today, something it desperately wants to do, something that if it SOA were applied would then become viable. An example of this might be as simple as the current core banking application, authorization switch, claims application, Internet portal, or other must accommodate the ability to deliver new products within six months. This scenario would get elaborated until it was clear and agreed that there is a problem and change is required. Based on Figure 2.3, business scenarios are defined and elaborated for each goal that is a priority. If an alternative approach to SOA exists, each alternative is identified, weighed, and a decision made as to the most viable approach to deliver on the strategic business goals.

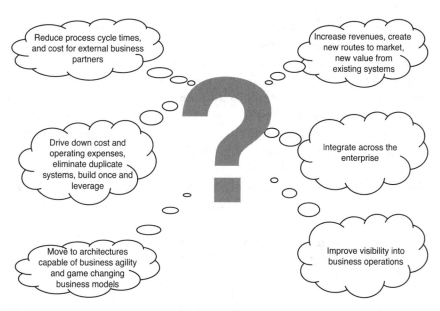

Figure 2.3   Basic reasons for SOA adoption

Selling SOA to the business is possible for organizations that fit the profile defined in Figure 2.4. Companies with executive leadership experienced in selling ideas and developing sound rationales and business cases for change are more likely to be successful at selling SOA directly as a strategic change agent. Companies that fit this profile are efficient in their use of IT, and the relationship with business and IT is one of trust and highly collaborative. These organizations measure what they are doing and track their improvement and maturity. They actually have a desire to improve, and as a result they invest in strategic opportunities that can change the business. Variable costs are present, which allows investment dollars to be applied. If a business case or ROI is required to make strategic purchases and the company does not have a mature dialogue with the business, any/all SOA purchases may not be approved. Organizations that can sell SOA can make purchases of hardware and software, run pilots, and conduct benchmarks, to determine the suitability of new architectural approaches to their business. Business cases replace ROI analysis, and the business case shows how one or more goals depicted in Figure 2.3 can be realized. Business cases, which show a high probability of creating increased or sustained business value, are favored over in-depth analysis in making a strategic decision.

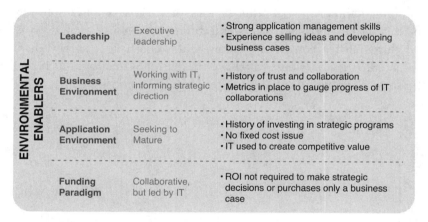

Figure 2.4   Profile for environment suited to selling SOA

When neither of the approaches above is practical or workable, but to a visionary or leader it is clear that SOA adoption would be of value, a focus on business as usual is in order. That is, justify a project as before using ROI, business value analysis, or business case. When a project has been approved, it should then be evaluated for SOA suitability. If the project is suitable, consider the project strategic and tactical goals to identify specific potential SOA benefits. The final step may involve persuading and educating both business and IT project teams as to why the project's strategic goals can be enhanced with SOA adoption.

8. What Is the Return on Investment (ROI) of SOA Adoption?

Early SOA adopters have not focused on measuring return for SOA because bigger, more-profound forces are impacting decisions: how to change the ratio of IT spend so that more is spent on innovation rather than costs, how to make strategic applications more flexible, how to deliver faster value to the business, how to be more responsive to their customers and markets, and how to improve business performance.

Figure 2.5 shows that without SOA the long-term cost of the IT solution to the business will be higher. There are several reasons for non-SOA solutions having a higher cost, with the most prevalent being that non-SOAs don't have flexibility built in (as described in detail in Chapter 6). SOA reduces the lifetime cost of an IT solution, and this is a key ROI metric. Several studies by vendors, analyst firms, and third parties consistently show that when asked, surveyed, or evaluated, 100% of clients who have successful SOA adoptions report and show improved flexibility, another key ROI metric.

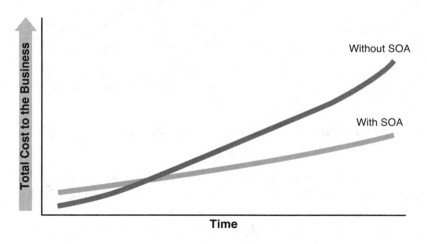

Figure 2.5   Total cost to the business with and without SOA

The upside of SOA is that the cost of building new applications drops as services are deployed and the service-reuse rate climbs. The catch is that there's a significant ramp-up cost, because adopting an SOA means organizations need to rethink traditional approaches to application management. The cost savings of SOA extend beyond application management as fewer software licenses and servers translate into cost savings in capital and operating budgets. Fewer redundant software components translates into less need for people for support. Application consolidation onto fewer platforms reduces software life cycle costs. SOA will require more upfront investment, and for organizations focused solely on tactical concerns, this is problematic because investments are often not available as tactics trump strategy and planning for the future.

Measuring return for IT solutions is notoriously difficult, and some companies see ROI as limiting, others guess at ROI, and still others spend so much time on ROI that they lose precious time to create value along the way. However, everyone agrees that measurement is necessary, or rather that there must be some business value return. Increased competition, rising costs, and limited budgets are not unique to any industry. All industries must make difficult decisions about where and how to invest limited capital. However, organizations must make decisions that impact the organization's long-term viability to be efficient, cost-effective, and flexible while being attentive to the marketplace. Organizations must deal with competing pressures to develop practical plans for IT investments.

Although difficult, various measurements can be used to determine an ROI on IT solutions. Some of the measurements can be viewed as delivering hard, tangible monetary values, whereas others require a bit of finesse to truly measure the benefits in financial terms. Nevertheless, it is important to document both tangible and intangible benefits and use the results in the process of measuring or estimating the ROI on any SOA adoption. Decisions to invest in SOA should not be driven solely by ROI calculations, but by broader determinations on what investment best delivers on both strategic and tactical concerns.

9. How Should the Business Measure the Effectiveness of SOA?

Many companies approach SOA with unbridled expectations accompanied with few if any measurements of success. SOA projects are perceived to have failed (or worse, SOA is perceived to have failed) when in fact there is no way to measure or track success; and in most cases, the organizations have not started SOA adoption but have merely purchased software labeled as SOA and done web services adoptions. The multifaceted nature of SOA value proposition requires measuring effectiveness because the value varies greatly from one project to another and from one line of business to the next.

Looking at SOA value propositions and defining corresponding metrics for each value proposition is necessary to measure the effectiveness of SOA. Organizations should already be tracking, assessing, and improving their organization's efficiency and effectiveness using metrics. Organizations with minimal experience in measurement programs may struggle with identifying and tracking measurements for SOA. Organizations must master metrics that assist with continuous improvement, addressing business or client partner satisfaction, solution quality, project implementations delivered on time, production defects introduced per person year, number of defects within 30 days of implementation, and project dollars actual to budget. Organizations will see value in adopting the Capability Maturity Model Integration (CMMI) as a process-improvement approach that improves their performance, although this is not required.

Measuring the effectiveness of SOA starts with identifying specific value propositions and assigning a suitable metric for assessing and tracking. When looking at effectiveness, the following value propositions are viable and potential metrics:

- **Improve IT's ability to respond to the businesses needs**
  Metrics: Reduced calendar time to deploy new solutions, increase in types of changes business stakeholders (non-IT) can make, opportunity value related to faster time to market

- **Speed up delivery time**
  Metrics: Reduced hours or % of development schedule, reduced test cycles or time

- **Improve flexibility of applications**
  Metrics: % reduction in life cycle time from concept to production, elapsed days a functional type changes (e.g., regulatory rules) can be deployed into production, number of changes that business users can make or deploy, speed of moving through test environments

- **Improve flexibility of business processes**
  Metrics: Number of processes that can be reconfigured, number of services being used, number of standard business processes

Measuring the efficiency of SOA also begins with identifying value propositions and assigning metrics. Efficiency measurements, like effectiveness metrics, require organizations to baseline data so that improvements can be measured and tracked. Common efficiency value propositions include the following:

- **Reduce the lifetime cost of applications**
  Metrics: Reduction in resources for maintaining code; reduction in cost for fixing code-related problems in production; reduction in number of defects, number of services being created, number of services being created with a single consumer

- **Reduce cost of integration**
  Metrics: Number of application using shared SOA infrastructure, integration cost avoided or reduced by production-deployed infrastructure, reduced cost of building interfaces and infrastructure to support application integration

- **Improve productivity**
  Metrics: Person days required to build a service, cost to build a service, project delivery times are shortening, number of projects being delivered, improvements in time to market for new capabilities

- **Reuse of SOA assets**
  Metrics: Number of services with multiple consumers, number of services being consumed, service reuse ratios

- **Support long-term sunset strategy for applications**
  Metrics: Number of common functions from multiple applications converted to services

In addition to the measurement approaches articulated, companies will benefit from defining a vision or strategy for SOA. Reaching consensus is at the core of an SOA vision (on, for example, the definition of SOA, the value propositions that must be addressed, business scenarios that reflect the need for the stated value propositions and the corresponding elaboration of how SOA will address the scenarios and enable the realization of the benefits, and the value propositions).

Using a maturity model provides guidance on what level of SOA maturity must be present to achieve a desired business value or value proposition.

Figure 2.6 shows a high-level overview of an SOA maturity model, referred to as the Service Integration Maturity Model (SIMM).[1] This model is the basis of a standard named the Open Group Service Integration Maturity Model (OSIMM).[2] Organizations can use the maturity model to determine what business value is desired, because each level of the maturity model has distinct value propositions that can be achieved. For example, if the value proposition is around reducing the lifetime cost of applications, level 5 would be the required maturity level in several domains: business, organization, methods, applications, architecture, information, and infrastructure. However, if the value proposition were solely around optimizing a business process with external partners, achieving level 2, maturity, in a few domains would suffice.

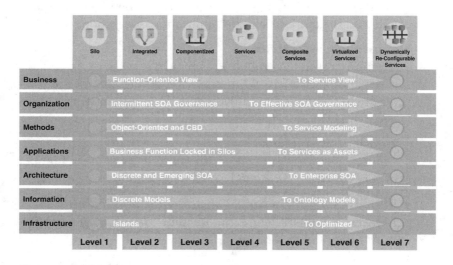

Figure 2.6   SOA maturity model

---

[1] See http://www.ibm.com/developerworks/webservices/library/ws-soa-simm/ for a description.

[2] See http://www.opengroup.org/pubs/catalog/c092.htm.

Although it is beyond the scope of this question (and book) to describe the SIMM or OSIMM, you can use such models to provide a measurable roadmap as to where the organization is and where it needs to be. The maturity model differs from many traditional maturity models in a few ways, one being that a maturity level, when reached, reflects a capability that the business has obtained versus a process improvement. So, the maturity model does not reflect increasing maturity of any specific action or activities that an organization performs, but instead reflects a capability or business outcome. Reducing the lifetime cost of an application is an example of a business outcome that can be measured, whereas being able to reconfigure business processes without IT development is a capability that can be measured.

10. What Are the Criteria for Selecting a Project for SOA Adoption?

SOA is not a one-size-fits-all solution. Chapter 6 examines the types of applications that are best suited for SOA. To answer this question, we first look at whether SOA is being pursued as an architectural direction or whether the SOA is largely focused on the use of services. SOA as an architectural approach requires the use of services, but the use of services does not require an architectural direction.

When an organization sees efficiency or effectiveness issues with IT or application management, it's a good reason to examine whether SOA can make a difference. Therefore, all projects that create strategic assets or have the intent to differentiate or change the business should be candidates for SOA adoption. Whenever an organization embarks on projects to address any of the strategic concerns listed in Question 6, it should pursue SOA adoption as part of that project. Figure 2.7 describes characteristics of projects suitable for SOA. For projects that have a high rate of change (e.g., business rules, business models, or process models), if the change rate is high, infusing change as an attribute is a key architecture benefit of SOA. Organizations experiencing project slippages because of shared business functionality benefit from reuse of functionality, and such projects are also good candidates for SOA. Projects with a business-process or external-partner focus and projects where business functionality, objects, are dispersed and usage is horizontally required are suitable projects for SOA adoption. When organizations are adopting standardized processes across existing silos, SOA provides a means, using services, to share functionality and at the same time have variances based on geographic or other boundaries. Lastly, strategic assets require the most flexibility, and using SOA as the architecture blueprint for creating such assets can result in long-range and sustained business benefits.

Most Suitable for SOA	Suitability Characteristics	Unlikely SOA Case
	Business Characteristics	
High	Business Process Change Rate	Low
High	Reuse of Functionality	Low
Process Oriented	Transactional Model	System Oriented
Horizontal	Organizational Scope	Vertical
Distributed	Business Objects	Centralized
Yes	Strategic Asset	No

Figure 2.7   Projects suitable for SOA adoption

11. What Is Flexibility and How Does SOA Deliver on This Promise?

Flexibility has become essential for many organizations as they navigate highly volatile, increasingly complex environments. Companies must be able to respond to myriad changes. After all, customers are increasingly demanding, globalization continues, information overload is a real threat, and economic power and innovation are rapidly shifting to developing markets. As the marketplace globalizes, new markets, new workforces, and new competitors force companies to look for ways to adapt more quickly. Flexibility is the capacity to adapt.

Information technology provides capabilities that enable and improve flexibility, and at the same time IT may be the source of inflexibility and the inability of organizations to adapt as quickly as their markets demand. Flexibility, like SOA, often has an identity crisis, as definitions are elusive and situational. Specific elements of IT have been cited as sources of flexibility, whether it is new technologies that make possible more agile financial modeling, mobile devices that capture data at point of origin and thus improve efficiency, or development of applications that improve business effectiveness. Arcane architectures create roadblocks for flexibility, and ever-evolving modern architectures like SOA increase flexibility. Architecture becomes a tool that makes a positive improvement to an organization's or a company's flexibility, its ability to adapt.

In the past, companies often had linear business processes that were handled by an individual department within a company. As sophistication increased, we saw the same business processes being broken up and pieces of it being performed in different places. For example, customers placed orders directly through the Web, services were shared by different parts of the company (e.g., merchandising or the supply chain took over at a certain step in the process), suppliers contributed vendor-managed inventory, and shipping was outsourced. This kind of disaggregation requires significant flexibility to establish and even more to change after it gains a foothold. SOA creates flexibility by allowing for flexible business processes that can readily be changed or reconfigured to suit the needs of the business.

So, flexibility in the context of IT as an enabler can be viewed in three contexts: time, efficiency, and effectiveness. In each context, the organization can potentially gain agility. Cycle time shrinking in business processes is a change. In the past, companies may have made significant changes yearly, but flexibility is when the same level of change can be realized on a monthly or even weekly or daily basis. So, flexibility can be defined and measured as how fast a change can be deployed into production. SOA helps make changes faster. The "how" has been partially addressed in Question 9, and is fully addressed when we cover organizations, applications, methods, architectures, and infrastructures in later chapters.

While business leaders may focus on cost containment, growth will also be on the agenda, and growth demands the flexibility to be more nimble than competitors. However, fueling growth requires businesses to look for ways to optimize current investments. This might necessitate increasing reuse of assets (application, business functions housed within applications, and infrastructure), reducing costs, or improving productivity, In other words, flexibility is about efficiency. SOA provides the architectural blueprint for increasing reuse by focusing on organizational reuse and organizational change as a critical success

factor. SOA provides the architectural underpinning for reusing infrastructure and for decoupling applications from hardware and software,
allowing old and hard-to-maintain software to be easily replaced when
needed and thus avoiding the IT inflexibility of earlier approaches.

Organizations often find themselves changing their business models. For example, a company that has sold to other businesses and
consumers for decades may shift to selling only business to business.
Or one day, a credit card processor is handling credit cards only, but
the next day, it must handle debit and credit cards. Many architectures
are not up to the challenge of addressing both effectiveness and efficiency, which are vital to rapid product development to remain competitive. SOA, as an architecture, provides for both effectiveness and
efficiency.

Flexibility is a trait that companies seek and that IT enables. Flexibility can be viewed in the context of time, effectiveness, and efficiency. SOA more than earlier approaches improves all three
dimensions for an organization. When understood and realized, SOA
brings flexibility as an architectural trait.

12. How Is Reuse Accomplished Using SOA?

Organizations constantly face the challenge and conflicting pressures of keeping their existing processes and operations running
while at the same time updating their practices; after all, change is a
constant. Tactical concerns often take priority over strategic concerns,
and line management and project managers find it difficult to adopt
new practices. Reuse in the context of SOA is a new practice but
maintains the same challenges of adopting reuse present in earlier
attempts at reuse. What is new is that SOA focuses on getting business stakeholders and IT stakeholders to reuse assets called services,
where services are business assets that get consumed, configured, and
assembled (that is, *reused*). However, the focus is not on developers
as was the case with object-oriented development, the focus is on the
business and getting the business to reuse business services.

Services have a service interface, a contract that decouples the consumer of the service from the provider of the service. The clients,
requestors, or consumers of the service do not need to understand the

technology or inner workings of the service, they just need to know the contract. The service operates as a black box, almost like an appliance. Services represent business function and provide an architectural environment where reuse can thrive. Later chapters in this book describe in more detail activities that must be performed to maximize and enable reuse. SOA make reuse more possible, more viable, through the notion of a service as a black box of business functionality that can easily be accessed with new facades as technology changes. Today, those facades might be the web based (e.g., cloud computing), mobile devices, people, or other systems. Tomorrow, it might be virtual worlds, 3D devices, the spoken Web, or other technologies yet to be created.

SOA does not eliminate existing barriers to reuse that are largely organizational issues. Reuse requires a change in process. Successfully implemented, wide-scale reuse addresses four key activities:

- Planning, funding, and prioritization of reusable assets
- The development of reusable assets
- Certification, maintenance, classification, and packaging of reusable assets
- The actual reuse

SOA requires a planning process, which includes establishing a strategy or vision for how SOA and services will make a difference. Services, which by design are reusable, must be identified, funded, and prioritized. Service development must occur and address service granularity and the overall design of the service. Services should have their own life cycle, which means that services are certified that they have gone through the necessary test cycles and can be deployed into production and produce predicable results when consumed. Service reuse is facilitated with technologies that aid in the discovery of services.

13. What Should the Business or Business Stakeholders Do Differently Because of SOA?

Effective SOA requires strong business stakeholder support, management support, and buy-in. Joint business and IT solution teams can make a huge difference in creating improved outcomes for

IT projects. When both stakeholders have a vested and partnership role, SOA adoption becomes easier. This translates to having a business leader responsible for business performance and who has a role in establishing a company's vision/strategy for SOA. Business stakeholders who might be business architects or business analysts will assume additional roles for business service visioning and planning. They will help identify reusable business services and the business scenarios that maximize consumption, service reuse. This will be accomplished with an eye toward business value and where that is best achieved. So, if not currently being performed, business stakeholders will increase their partnership with IT such that business and IT activities are intertwined and the leadership teams operate almost interchangeably.

Funding mechanisms and prioritization of projects are processes that exist in every organization. Both processes may need tweaking to accommodate SOA, because the notions of service funding and service owners are business concerns when services are viewed and treated as business assets. The change for business and business stakeholders is to address how new services are funded and then funding for maintenance (break/fix), enhancements, and other life cycle concerns for services. Service owners will be required to address certification of a service, making sure it has satisfied a required set of tests before deployment into production.

Identification of business services is a major change for business and business stakeholders. Business plays a crucial role in helping to identify services and using services as the basis for release planning, scope management, and requirements gathering. Instead of pushing functional requirements to IT to satisfy, sort, and interpret, business and IT will work collaboratively to identify a catalog of services needed by release.

Figure 2.8 shows different buckets that represent requirements. Another change with business stakeholders is to begin to think of requirements not as one thing but as a series of different things, buckets. Each bucket must be filled as soon as it's known what needs to go into the bucket. However, separating the buckets will facilitate flexibility, because requirements will have less of the how and will focus instead on the what. For example, the business process model will be understood, captured, documented, and maintained as a separate artifact by business stakeholders. This model will be used to populate another bucket, the list of business services in a service model. Rules and policies will be identified and separated into different buckets, allowing for improved agility, because we might want to identify which business rules should be business stakeholder manipulated and production deployable. The use case model that captures functional requirements will be built from the candidate business services. Information, workflow, and the user experience will comprise yet another set of buckets. Technical requirements for business services such as response time will also be captured, and external interface requirements will be captured in a system context bucket.

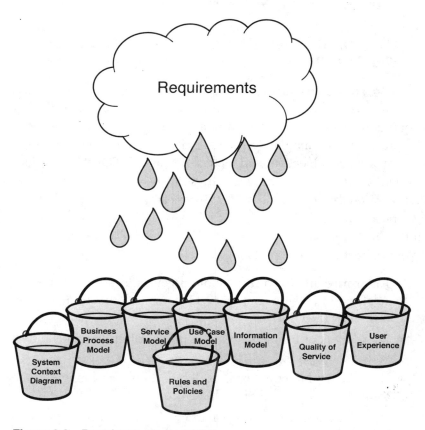

Figure 2.8   Requirements and SOA

The separation of requirements into different buckets moves organizations away from silos because we no longer create requirements for applications. Instead, we define requirements for the user experience, requirements for shared business services, and perhaps shared business rules and policies. So, the process by which business and IT communicate about requirements changes with SOA, and the business maintains some artifacts around requirements, such as process models. This means the application will no longer dictate what the business does; the business will dictate what applications must do. Business stakeholders will use process models as one input to communicate what the process should be doing now and in the future. IT working with business will digitize aspects of the process model using services, where services become strategic business assets.

14. Can SOA Be Applied to Business Architecture or Should It Be Used Solely for IT?

There are many definitions of *business architecture,* and the term is used by various organizations differently. The Object Management Group defines business architecture as "a blueprint of the enterprise that provides a common understanding of the organization and is used to align strategic objectives and tactical demands." TOGAF describes business architecture as "the business strategy, governance, organization, and key business processes." Historically, business architecture has appeared within the context of enterprise architecture. However, addressing business architecture as only a piece of traditional enterprise architecture can be problematic:

- Enterprise architecture in some organizations is perceived as solely an IT activity, something IT does, and something led and owned by the CIO.
- Developers of business architecture are often IT stakeholders versus business.
- Business architecture is considered simply a stepping stone toward developing an IT architecture.
- Business stakeholders don't participate in enterprise architecture or business architecture development, thus minimizing the effectiveness of the resulting business architecture.

In some organizations, the debate about which groups own the business architecture also hinders its effectiveness. After all, ideally, business should own the content of the business architecture and its relevancy, while development and maintenance of business architecture artifacts should be the responsibility of the group with the most qualified resources in terms of domain and artifact creation knowledge.

When well defined and developed collaboratively with the proper business and IT stakeholders, business architecture can guide organizations investments in terms of what to retire, where to invest, what to commoditize, and where opportunities for revenue may best lie. Business architecture can provide new business insights and uncover unforeseen opportunities. The problem today for many organizations is that they are hard-wired to existing business functions and IT systems and infrastructure, making change expensive and time-consuming. Organizational complexity compounds the problem, making cost savings difficult to achieve. SOA can be applied to the business and to business architecture to address these challenges.

When examined through the lens of IT, SOA provides a discrete package of business functions with a defined role, having a defined purpose with explicit duties and responsibilities, called services. SOA when examined from the lens of business that partitions its operations into nonoverlapping components, modeling the theme of SOA, further enabling reuse in the business and thereby maximizing optimization. Each component (business component such as a service) represents a persistent capability or business function. Traditional business process models reflect repetitive behavior that can be streamlined or automated. A business component looks from a different perspective to identify the ingredients of business that work together or in various combinations in business operations. Each business component has a unique and discrete role, resulting in a separation of concerns. This allows the business and stakeholders to identify opportunities to reduce cost where multiple business processes/applications, for examples, are used in a single business component. The business can also see better opportunities to differentiate or increase revenue by looking at the business through this new lens. SOA (and hence, service-oriented thinking) is about separation of concerns and breaking things into nonoverlapping parts that allow for optimization.

15. What Are the Common Pitfalls from a Business Vantage Point in Adopting SOA?

Most companies that have chosen SOA for one or more application management concerns have created their own definitions of SOA. This is problematic because it often means competing definitions, poor metrics (if any) to measure success, and of course, no guiding vision as to how the architecture will solve the problems of effectiveness or efficiency mentioned earlier in this chapter. Many companies are still on a journey to improve dialogue between IT and business and mistakenly believe SOA can help them reach their intended destination without organization change and governance.

IT governance programs are in place in many organizations. SOA governance is an afterthought for some organizations, although most organizations understand that SOA success requires SOA governance. However, many organizations have not fundamentally changed their ability to respond to the business as a result of SOA, largely because of ineffective SOA governance, competing SOA definitions within the organization, and little to no measurement program. Very few organizations have metrics to legitimize SOA investments and to demonstrate progress resulting from SOA.

For several companies, existing application management issues are accompanied by the inability to mandate a strategy (one that includes SOA) to address these issues. Companies are struggling with service identification and granularity largely because of the failure to embrace method changes to existing system development methods. Often, these same companies relegate SOA to specific types of projects and haven't implemented SOA across the enterprise.

Complex application environments force many companies to perform wrapping and interfacing while not addressing reusable business services. Companies are consolidating their application portfolio, while transforming their system development life cycles, without enhancing their methods to include SOA principles, artifacts, or best practices.

Organizational change takes a backseat in many SOA governance programs. For example, companies spent a lot of time training IT staff about SOA and limited time educating business personnel about SOA capabilities. Governance efforts haven't been effective in changing the business perception of SOA, and the absence of organizational change and the dearth of respected champions of SOA compounds the problem.

Business: Key Concepts

Business stakeholders should be interested in SOA and care about its adoption for many reasons. Flexibility is important to all organizations, and IT is a tool that can help organizations attain flexibility. Organizations that recognize a need to be more responsive to their markets, want to leverage that responsiveness to be more profitable, increase market share, and improve customer loyalty (all scenarios that represent improvements in business outcomes) and that are prepared to leverage their IT capabilities to achieve these advantages should care about SOA. SOA is the architecture choice for agility.

Organizations pursuing business or IT transformation, seeking faster time to value from IT, trying to modernizing strategic applications, attempting to lower the lifetime cost of applications or infrastructure, trying to do more for less, pursuing reuse as a goal to bring products or capabilities to the market faster, and looking to make flexibility a strategic capability should understand and pursue SOA adoption.

3

Organization

There is a potentially infectious condition inside virtually all organizations that can cause more damage than economic downturns, management upheavals, or global business shifts. Until now it has no name. But this condition has been an enormous problem in all facets of business...

I call it the "fiefdom syndrome," and it happens to all organizations, large and small, profit and non profit. It occurs at the individual level as well. And it can significantly decrease an individual's, and a company's, effectiveness.

The fiefdom syndrome stems from the inclination of managers and employees to become fixated on their own activities, their own careers, their own territory or turf to the detriment of those around them.

People who tend to hoard resources. They are determined to do things their own way, often duplicating or complicating what should be streamlined throughout the company, leading to runaway costs, increased bureaucracy, and slower response times.

—Robert J Herbold, *The Fiefdom Syndrome*

By now, everyone who has launched SOA projects or attended SOA conferences or read the numerous articles and book knows that organizational issues are as important as technical issues for achieving many SOA goals. Many of the organizational issues that impede meeting SOA goals relate to governance, its presence or absence; but another set of issues relates to behavior and culture—organizational issues. Several of these issues reflect the fiefdom syndrome, where lines of business, divisions, or departments within a company avoid sharing, battle against standardization, and resist change. The fiefdom syndrome can be seen as politics or turf wars, but for many trying to make SOA promises real, addressing the fiefdom syndrome seems like trying to boil an ocean. Anticipating organizational issues and preparing ahead of time with effective approaches is essential to success in SOA. Organizational issues matter, and this chapter provides answers for the various questions we have addressed on several projects:

16. How does business/IT alignment change because of SOA?
17. Which joint business/IT processes change because of SOA?
18. What organizational structures should be established for SOA?
19. What is the role of organizational change management to SOA?
20. How can organizational barriers to SOA success be removed?
21. How should organizations address funding for services?
22. How should organizations address prioritization for shared services?
23. What is the value of classifying services?
24. Who owns service reuse?
25. What are service owners?
26. What are the common organizational pitfalls when adopting SOA?

Organization: Q&A

16. How Does Business/IT Alignment Change Because of SOA?

The alignment between business and IT in most organizations lies on a continuum between highly collaborative and tense. This is not unusual given that all relationships involving people, money, and commitments can create a highly collaborative environment or one of mistrust and tension. SOA provides the opportunity for a middle ground, where both the business and IT get what they have sought:

business gets new levels of flexibility, while IT reaps the rewards of a uniform architecture built for change. Application development by the consumers of services can occur without waiting in long IT development queues by the provider of services; the decoupling of the IT side from the business side through services and a federated architecture makes this possible. SOA changes and improves the relationship between business and IT as a result of shared services. For bank debit or credit accounts, transfer funds are built once as reusable services regardless of whether access is through a call center, web interface, or mobile device. For insurance companies, submit loan application or perform claims adjudication; for telecommunication carriers, get location information; and across all industries, get account information and update customer address are not functions built many times because of silo applications, silo organizations, or different access channels, but shared services that are built once and reused. The strategy shifts to a reuse, buy and build versus buy and build.

Improving the relationship between business and IT does not occur magically or without planning. Figure 3.1 illustrates the general range of business and IT relationships, where unified is a desired state.

In the unified state, people come together as teams for collaboration, problem solving, portfolio management, project prioritization, and governance. Stakeholders don't wear hats called business or IT when they meet because they know these labels don't reflect the breadth of their contributions. Business stakeholders increasingly provide suggestions about IT, and IT stakeholders provide business insights; each side plays an integral partnership role in the success of the organization.

In the synced state, teams are formed to work on problems. However, the team often dissolves when the problem is considered "solved." Organizational reporting hierarchies often take precedence over domain knowledge in selecting team members. Governance is maturing in the sync state and there is a lot of conversation on how to improve and align business and IT. Organizational change is discussed but material changes have yet to take effect that change behavior between business and IT.

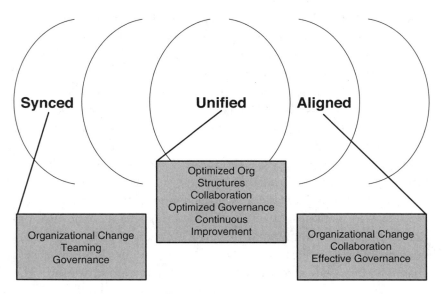

Figure 3.1   Business and IT relationship states

A collaborative environment with effective governance characterizes the aligned state. Business and IT alignment is a mantra often echoed when looking at how to improve business and IT relationships. Using a standards- and service-based approach where a service repository can be used as a central authority (much like databases do for information) changes business and IT relationships into a service. Like data that becomes a common language, a business language develops between business and IT. Regardless of whether organizations find themselves at the unified, aligned, or sync level of maturity, when services becomes a business and IT term, there is an opportunity for improved dialogue between business and IT. In addition, collaboration and sharing increase when designing and constructing the shared services.

Unified is an optimal state for business and IT relationships, it represents a convergence of business and IT, a partnership. The relationships of a unified state are not born without hard labor, but the result is a highly collaborative environment built on trust. Organizational structures are continually optimized to create operational dexterity that allows organizations to be more agile. Governance is active, effective, and tweaked continuously using measurements and feedback loops. Continuous improvement to measure, tweak, and monitor is a way of life. Reaching this unified state of relationship between business and IT is a goal of SOA adoption that occurs incrementally from sync to align to unify.

17. Which Joint Business/IT Processes Change Because of SOA?

Several joint business/IT processes change as a result of SOA including: governance, portfolio management, strategic planning, managing investments, requirements gathering, and project prioritization. These changes are as follows:

- Governance is collaborative. Both business and IT stakeholders are inserted into existing processes related to how projects are funded, and when projects are built, bought, extended, or reused as business functionality. Each and every governance process should be examined with an eye toward establishing/enhancing collaborative roles between business and IT.

- Portfolio management is in place to avoid the proliferation of services and applications. "Less is more" is the mantra, but this requires active management where both the business stakeholders responsible for the business operations and the IT stakeholders responsible for IT automation sit together to discuss how to extend, retire, provision, or reuse an existing services portfolio of shared business services. Reuse becomes a priority versus buying or building from scratch.

- Strategic planning addresses sharing across the organization for increased business operational flexibility. Sharing of services and its enabling infrastructure occurs regardless of whether the organization represents a centralized or decentralized IT delivery model. Issues pertaining to standardized business processes are addressed as the return of investment of the overall organization is favored over the investment of a single business unit.

- Managing funding for how sharing of services is either promoted or governed. In some cases, "business as usual" cost allocation and funding models work, and for other organizations these models must be enhanced. Success of shared services should justify increased investments.

- Requirements gathering also change how business and IT interact and relate when specifying requirements. Practices that promote application silos give way to practices that promote the strategy of "build once and reuse." This requires a twofold approach: providing a view into what can be reused at the business level during requirements gathering and moving away from specifying requirements as functional domains, which is largely done today with use case modeling. The change around requirements is discussed in more detail in Chapter 5, "Methods."

- Project prioritization takes into consideration the shared functionality necessary for the on-time, on-budget delivery of projects. Globalization, increased competition, and empowered customers force a choice about what to do first. Services such as applications must be part of any prioritization scheme.

Each of these changes occurs incrementally based on the strategic and tactical goals for adopting SOA. Meeting the strategic goals of SOA ultimately, and for the promises of SOA to be fulfilled, requires reaching the unified stage depicted in Figure 3.1.

18. What Organization Structures Should Be Established for SOA?

Most organizations are structured to support product lines or vertical business units with IT organized accordingly, often with application teams aligned to the vertical lines of business. People, skills, and budgets are focused on discrete projects prioritized by the line of business. At the same time, an increasing number of projects need to share a business function created in another line of business. For example, in banking there may be divisions of retail, wholesale, credit cards, and loans. Shared information about a customer and shared business capability such as update address or get account information are needed by retail, wholesale, credit card, and loans. Different lines of business, different departments need access to discrete units of business functionality without building bridges (i.e., interfaces) or sitting in development queues waiting for access to be delivered. That is, shared services are needed and on the rise, and how companies organize themselves can make a difference.

Figure 3.2 illustrates a typical organizational structure in most large companies that have both business units and a separate IT department. Business units or lines of business typically have an application development team assigned to support their business unit residing in the IT department. In some organizations, a hybrid may exist where development resources are found both in the business unit and IT. Sitting in the IT department are often relationship managers, executives, who report to the CIO and who have a dotted-line report to a business unit executive who is peer to the CIO. This relationship manager has a deep understanding of the business unit and is responsible for the IT automation needs of their business units. Business analysts or business architects often report into this area. Application development teams are in the IT department. These are often silo and centralized teams that provide support, database administration, network engineering, infrastructure, operations, security, and in some organizations, enterprise architecture (EA).

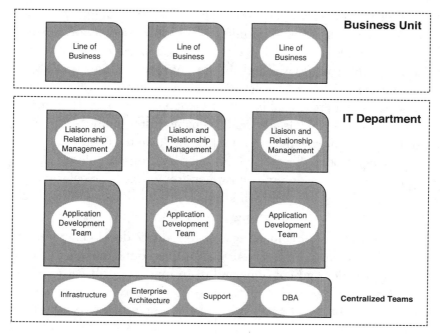

Figure 3.2   Typical IT organizational structure

The debate for many organizations about what should change for SOA often centers on whether there should be a centralized team for service development and what the role of an EA team is. Centralized teams for service development may make sense on a transient or permanent basis. Often, organizations have limited skills and resources for the architecture, design, and building of services, and centralizing this capability under a shared pool works to resolve this resource constraint. However, conflict can arise between the consumer and provider roles for services. That is, the domain knowledge to build the service is often found within the current application development teams supporting the business units, yet the development role has been removed from this team and centralized. Accountability issues ensue as the consumer becomes the application team and the provider becomes the centralized team. Finger pointing can occur around requirements and delivery as application teams have a major responsibility removed, which is building out the functionality required to support their business units.

A distinction exists between organizations pursuing factory models versus organizations centralizing the development of services. Factory models are often desired because organizations want to take advantage of a flat world and the advantages of a 24x7 clock or a cheaper work force. Examples are seen as companies move work to labor pools that are available with lower labor costs. In service development, factory models are used to enable faster and less-expensive service development. In both a factory model and a centralized service delivery model, clearly defined roles and responsibilities regarding the service provider and consumer are needed. Typically, factory models work best when only limited aspects of the service life cycle are assigned to the factory: programming and unit testing.

Organizations implementing a shared service development model want to avoid creating a fragmented project accountability model with unclear provider and consumer roles. In most cases, because of the domain knowledge and direct access to the service consumers, it makes sense for the provider role to be accountable for all aspects of service delivery. Application teams should have a provider role, and any fragmentation or diffusion of this role using centralized teams should be temporary or account for how project delivery accountability will be resolved so as not to create an inefficiency in the development of shared services. Understanding and defining the role of service owners can help to resolve these issues because the service owner has a provider role with distinct responsibilities.

Shared service development models often fail because of fragmented and shared accountability on the responsibilities for creating a reusable service. Often the "blame game" becomes prominent, as the shared service development team does not have project accountability. The shared service team may blame the consumer (aka application) for not providing adequate requirements, domain knowledge, or any number of reasons. It's one of the main reasons why applications dislike using shared services; they give up control. It is crucial that there be a project accountability that reaches across all groups, and in which slippages are known by all immediately, with corresponding risk mitigation. If shared service development models are used, both groups must "have skin in the game," and operate under a single project management structure.

A modified IT organization structure for shared services is depicted in Figure 3.3, which shows two major changes to the traditional IT model: a business-focused role for an EA group and a centralized integration center. The EA team in many organizations today is largely IT focused and invisible to the business units. In the SOA world, the EA team must evolve from a primarily technical focus to a fused business and technical focus. The EA team is responsible for enterprise architecture, working closely with the business and IT as a part of that EA responsibility to identify and promote shared services across the enterprise that can be used across multiple business units. EA also works closely with the liaison and relationship executive to understand business processes that span multiple units and promotes the sharing of business process design and their corresponding shared services, rules, and information. Standards for services are also a key responsibility of the EA team.

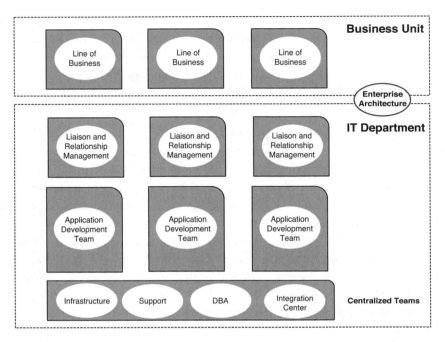

Figure 3.3   Modified IT organizational structure for shared services

The centralized integration center is responsible for addressing the business unit and their corresponding application team's vertical and horizontal integration needs using an *enterprise service bus* (ESB). The integration center has responsibility for architecture, design, development, and implementation of an ESB. This includes the development of message flows, mediation, routing, and transformation using the ESB and a registry. The integration center collaborates with the application development teams for service development and reuse. This collaboration is shown in Figure 3.4. The integration center defines and implements standards, guidelines, and processes for the ESB and registry. Facilitation of all aspects of ESB governance rests with the integration center working closely with application development teams. The integration center and application teams have joint responsibility for understanding and developing requirements for services. The application teams, possibly including a shared service application team as discussed previously, develop business services for use by the various business units and work with the integration team to satisfy integration needs within their silos (vertical) or integration needs that span business units (horizontal). Application teams also develop the business applications that compose or orchestrate or otherwise use the services. The integration center develops the necessary mediation, routing, or transformation features or services and publishes all services using the registry so that they are easily and readily accessible using an ESB.

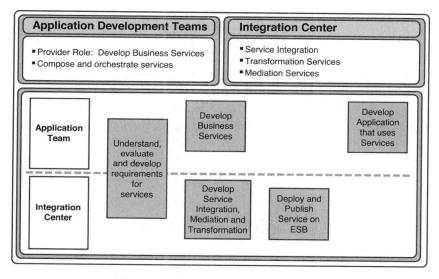

Figure 3.4   Business and IT relationship

Three organization models available for the integration center need to be evaluated against change management goals for the organization, people, and process. One option is to pool resources without concern for vertical domain knowledge or focus. The disadvantages of this option are the team may not be able to be as responsive as a vertically aligned team due to lack of access to subject matter expertise. This option might also create a bottleneck of the integration center because all requests have to be threaded through this single team Another option is to vertically align the integration center resources along business unit boundaries specializing in the subject area. However, this has the disadvantage of promoting silos, resulting in more duplication of effort and ultimately demanding more resources than other options. The third option is a hybrid, which is to have a vertical-based structure where the subject matter expertise lives and allows for vertical areas (business units) to quickly respond to their constituent needs. In the hybrid model, the integration center has largely technical resources skilled in how to build web services, leverage the ESB, and build services for routing, transformation, and mediation. Note that these same three options and their disadvantages can be applied to a centralized service development team (discussed previously).

The integration center is akin to *database administration* (DBA) teams that have been around for decades. The message flows and supporting integration services (i.e., mediation, routing, and transformation) are similar to what a DBA function does working to create shared data models and databases. What DBAs do for data and information, integration centers do for services and their message flows. We use this analogy to illustrate that organizations already know how to make integration centers work. However, integration centers represent a change in organization models when adopting SOA, and the good news is we know they can work

19. What Is the Role of Organizational Change Management to SOA?

Organizational change management is the answer to how barriers to SOA success can be removed organizationally. Organizational change management is required when adopting new strategies, such as SOA, because it requires a change in how teams develop applications, relationships, and interactions between business units and IT and changes within IT departments as to how they interact. Figure 3.5 illustrates the elements that organizations must understand, assess, and perform to create cultural and behavioral changes necessary to fulfill many strategic SOA goals. Change management affects the organization, processes, and IT when adopting SOA. It requires that there be some strategic goals, defined at the executive level, around performance measures, efficiency, and effectiveness goals. Chapter 2, "Business," provides a laundry list of possible strategic goals and measures that can be used to drive organizational change. Ultimately, an assessment must be made about what is working today in the organization and what improvements must be made, and this is based on the demands of the strategy and marketplace and balanced by supply of resources, skills, people, and tools.

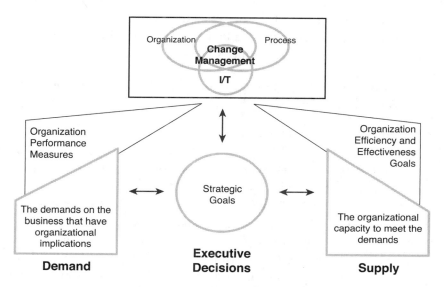

Figure 3.5   Fundamentals of organizational change management

   Change management is a well-established discipline, and organizations lacking expertise in how to start, assess, and implement change management should seek outside expertise. Communications is a key aspect and success factor for any strategic objective; the stakeholders get connected and updated before, during, and after the change initiative. For example, suppose the strategic goal is to improve integration both in efficiency (e.g., reduced cost of integration and improve productivity) and effectiveness (e.g., improve flexibility and respond faster to business demands). This goal has led to the adoption of an *enterprise service bus* (ESB), registry and shared services. Many in the IT department may not understand the difference between enterprise application integration versus using an ESB for service orientation. In the business units and their liaisons, resistance may exist to sharing services because they see a potential negative impact on the reliance of other teams outside control of their vertical business unit for project delivery. Others in the organization might not understand SOA, or they might have both negative and positive opinions about it. Still others might have seen the failure of past projects that promoted sharing of software assets. In each case, this points to the need for communication of the strategic objective before, during, and after the implementation of the ESB and its corresponding processes and organizational changes.

20. How Can Organizational Barriers to SOA Success Be Removed?

A battle rages among many circles as to who is holding SOA back, the business or IT. Of course, that depends on a lot of factors, but our experience shows that it varies by organization. In some IT departments, there is a heavy sell of SOA to the business, and it can work when there is trust and collaboration, often the result of business and IT consistently working collaboratively to produce noticeable and measurable business outcomes. In other IT departments, SOA just becomes another in a long series of lofty and unfulfilled promises. Chapter 1, "SOA Basics," provides answers about how to sell SOA to the business. Selling SOA is not about selling SOA but about selling how to achieve specific strategic and tactical goals of the business. Selling SOA can result in "shooting of the messenger," and the messenger might become a pariah; so it's advised not to sell SOA. However, thinking that expressing whether the business should be interested in SOA is the same as whether the business should be interested in Java or COBOL as a programming language is not correct. The choice of programming languages is strictly an IT concern; the adoption of SOA will require business and IT unification in using services for project scope management, requirements capture, and organizational reuse. Business stakeholders have a role in SOA adoption.

SOA is facing resistance as does all major shifts in human endeavors, and IT cannot escape this resistance. Resistance is found in leaders, executives, developers, and architects, and it's embedded in organizational models. Change occurs one death at a time. In the case of SOA, it might be the death of common practices, organizational models, or changing roles of key people. SOA continues to mean different things to different people, and this alone creates a barrier to success. The broken promises and platitudes surrounding

SOA have been used for decades, and cynicism and caution prevail. However, this again is directly related to whether organizations find themselves with a unified, aligned, or synced relationship between business and IT.

Breaking down barriers should start with defining a vision and strategy for how SOA will make a difference for an organization. Having a shared vision is integral to breaking down organizational barriers. This strategy should be grounded with the strategic and tactical goals facing lines of business and the enterprise and be accompanied by a practical and measurable roadmap for realizing the strategy. Selling SOA to the business is not recommended. Instead, projects should be identified and sought that are suitable for realizing both tactical and strategic goals of SOA. In addition, pursuing organizational change management can also make a huge difference in removing barriers.

Our experience also shows that sharing of services can be promoted and barriers broken down by conducting a facilitated workshop with the current and potential consumers. In the workshop, ask participants whether the workshop questions are answered satisfactory and if their concerns about sharing of services have been addressed. That is, if each question of concern were resolved, would the doubters support service sharing? Our experience shows that if a workshop is held addressing service funding, service prioritization, and service ownership using the inventory of questions provided in the next three questions, then resistance to sharing services is reduced. The workshop does not presume an answer to the questions; instead, it solicits the answers from the participants, the consumers and providers of services.

21. How Should Organizations Address Funding for Services?

Many practitioners adopting SOA see the lack of funding for shared services as a major bottleneck for SOA adoption. Two issues exist when discussing funding. The first issue is funding for shared services, where the first consumer may have to pay for subsequent consumers because the service has to be designed for reuse or will be reused. The second issue is where SOA needs a kick-start for funding related to governance, technology investments, or acquisition of new skills. Organizations have existing funding mechanisms, prior to SOA, for investment and for building business functionality; if these work and are effective, they should be modified and used for SOA adoption. So, existing and funding mechanisms that work should be used. The second issue centers on organizations that do not have investment funding for establishing governance, or shared infrastructures are disadvantaged when adopting SOA. In such cases, the shared infrastructure, governance, and other investments required for SOA adoption would need to be covered as part of project costs or buried in other investments.

Consider the issue of funding services for reuse. It is a risky business to build services with the mantra "if we build it, they will come," which is often the underlying assumption of building services for reuse. Business functionality when developed in an application should always consider the needs of the future, and change cases that depict future needs should be captured and prioritized as part of a requirements-gathering process. However, by definition, services can be reused, as explained further in the context of applications and methods in Chapter 5, "Methods," and Chapter 6, "Applications." A benefit of services is that by designing and deploying services in applications, organizations create applications that are built for change, with flexibility designed in the application architecture. This is a benefit for service regardless of whether a second consumer comes on board. However, having multiple consumers is also desired and a benefit. Having multiple consumers of a service that comprise multiple verticals is a selling point, business benefit, and design point for service development. However, in this case, service funding is not onerous because the business benefit becomes clear to both consumers. The challenge then becomes how do we convince the consumers that their needs will be met when they may have different time horizons for delivery of functional needs or different quality of service attributes (for example, underwriting needs three seconds performance but claims it is okay with five seconds)? Often the first creator of a service sees SOA as being built on the backs of their projects because they are designing services for reuse or they are designing services for use by other consumers. Both issues are best addressed as part of organizational change management, dealing with how to make the service creator have a benefit in addition to the service consumer with the creation of services.

Dependencies on other groups exist today for application and project teams, and clearly this will increase with services, where funding is just one of many dependencies. Organizations must determine how to make this increased collaboration work, instead of abandoning the notion of moving to shared services. Service funding concerns can be addressed by answering the following questions:

- Who pays for new services?
- Who pays for a break fix?
- Who pays for service maintenance?
- Who pays for service enhancement?
- Who pays for the services' foundational aspects of hardware, software, database maintenance and any other foundational features necessary to deploy the service?

Each organization using a workshop will answer these questions differently based on their culture. For some organizations, the workshop will result in concluding that the consumer or requester of a new service should pay for the service, just as any new feature would be funded by the requesting organization. Break fix and maintenance is part of the ongoing cost of maintaining applications and services, and the provider of the service should incur this cost. Maintenance costs would not be shared because the provider operates as a software provider where some minimal staff must be kept for maintenance regardless of whether there was a second consumer. The provider is also motivated to repair any defects because the defects negatively impact the provider as well as the consumer. Service enhancement, whether it's for new business functionality or to make the service available 24x7 is also something that the requester should fund. Requestors will be motivated to use the service as-is or with enhancements because the time to market savings are present with reuse. The provider, as part of a new service or enhancement request, pays the foundational aspects of the service. This discussion and the decisions occur in the workshop.

What has not been answered is who pays for getting an organization started with understanding SOA, building out the infrastructure, acquiring new skills for service development, and applying new development and operational technologies. Some organizations have investment strategies where the funding challenge is resolved; others must sell the business to secure investment funding. Chapter 2 addresses the issues of selling SOA to the business and defining strategic and tactical measurable goals. Organizations have three options:

- Obtain and use investment funds.
- Fund as part of a business justification.
- Launch a skunks work project where the cost is absorbed as part of underspent funds or heroic efforts. A skunk work project is where a small team launches a project primarily for the sake of innovation. Typically, it involves volunteerism and highly motivated team members who want to prove a concept for the benefit of the organization.

Realizing reuse to achieve the efficiency and effectiveness of SOA goals described in Chapter 1 does require organizational change management and governance, and this does require investment funding. Most organizations can secure this funding with incremental SOA successes that achieve measurable and clear business benefits that are well publicized and used as goodwill for future investments in SOA adoption.

Clearly, IT departments must maintain an environment that minimizes short- and long-term costs of any initiative. Selecting the correct projects for applying SOA and provisioning the correct supporting infrastructure at the right time is also integral to effective cost management. In some cases, the technology benefits of adopting SOA are clear, and in other cases, especially when strategic goals are to be met (see Chapter 2), it's important to articulate, define, and measure the business benefits. IT departments can work with the business in the same way as prior to SOA to manage the IT portfolio and cost. Some organizations find they can reallocate maintenance funds to launch their SOA adoptions efforts.

22. *How Should Organizations Address Prioritization for Shared Services?*

Prioritizing services is integral to the success of SOA adoption. Consumers have multiple concerns when using a service for which they have no direct control for its development or deployment. To increase support for sharing services within an enterprise, you can ask the following questions about service prioritization:

- How do we make sure that the provider has sufficient capacity in terms of subject matter expertise to implement changes?
- How do we align priorities across multiple lines of business when one line of business depends on the service of another?
- How do we make lines of business accountable to maintain priorities/interlocks?
- Will it take longer to develop shared services?
- How do we prioritize enhancements?
- Can the provider accommodate the business request and needs based on my line- of-business schedule and budget?
- Will a request be compromised because the provider has multiple interests and consumers to satisfy?
- Is the ability to deliver faster and on time lost or impacted due to accommodating conflicting requirements, coordination challenges, or challenges in accommodating different *quality of service* (QoS) requirements, or because of dependency on an organization outside of the vertical?

The reason a service is delivered by a particular business unit should be because that unit has specific domain knowledge about the business rules, process, and information. This domain knowledge of the subject matter expert puts the vertical in the optimum position to deliver quickest. This requires that a portfolio management and project prioritization process span the enterprise versus one that is a silo. This addresses the issue of what features should be delivered first and in what sequence. It requires that service development be treated as a project, just like application development. Each of these questions has various answers, but the answers largely lie in existing project prioritization processes that can be enhanced for service development.

23. What Are Service Owners?

Service owners are the providers of services that support multiple consumers. The provider of a service should architect, design, develop, and deploy a service. Service owners are like application owners in that they facilitate the sharing of services. Assigning ownership to a service facilitates governance, and like data owners, service owners have a stewardship role for services. Deciding who the service owners are can often be accomplished by determining which business unit owns the data that the service renders. When data governance is poor, data stewardship is also lacking and the owner of the data may be undetermined. In this case, the service owner can be the primary user of the process that uses the service—the process owner. Deciding on service owners addresses the following questions:

- Who owns the service?
- What does it mean to own a service?
- What are the roles and responsibilities of a service owner?
- Does the owner have veto authority over changes to services?
- Does the service owner decide who can have access to a service?

Owning a service is being responsible for making sure the services are used and used in the way to give most benefit to the business. Owners of the service need to be directly aligned to the business owners of the associated business processes. How this is done in practice depends on the organization and its structures and goals. What is true in every case is that the focus of this role should shift to business knowledge, with support from IT, which plays a provider role for the service in its engineering and deployment. Service owners have distinct responsibilities:

- Publish and maintain software architecture for the service
- Maintain a release plan for the service
- Articulate the deployment environment to meet defined and published QoS attributes for the service
- Certify a service and publish test results and test scripts for the service
- Manage the full life cycle for the service

24. What Is the Value of Classifying Services?

Often, there is a categorization or labeling of services, whether they be described as business services, IT services, information services, or utility services. Grouping services can help with understanding the degree of reuse possibilities, the domain covered, the business area scope, or ownership model of a service. Governance and provider responsibilities can vary based on the classification. For example, business services may be assigned to business stakeholders as owners and IT services assigned to owners in the IT department. Categories can also define service domains, where a domain defines a set of related services that someone can own, maintain, support, and fund. If an organization has defined a taxonomy of services, the classification helps architects, designers, and developers understand the scope of functionality to include in a service to promote composition and reuse. Enterprise architects can help with classification, and it becomes a fast path into searching for services and leveraging architectural frameworks for the design and implementation of services.

Service classification or categorization helps to match service types to a business process model, to logical operational models, or to layered component models. For example, services could be divided into two categories of business and technical services, where business services map to business process models and technical services map to operational aspects (such as authentication and authorization engine) of the architecture.

- Business services of createStockOrder, submitLoanApplication, renewPolicy, checkOrderAvailability, transferFunds, getStockPrice
- Technical services of validateUser, checkPassword, auditEvent

Classifying services is useful if there is a downstream use, later in the service life cycle, for the classification and if a taxonomy for the classification is published and communicated. For example, business services is a category that could be further refined into four categories by granularity:

- Business process is a service that is an explicitly modeled and executed process consisting of other business services.

Examples are createStockOrder, submitLoanApplication, and renewPolicy.

- Business Transaction is a service that changes persistent state of business data or otherwise accomplishes a business action. Examples are checkOrderAvailability and transferFunds.

- Business Function is a service that accesses business function or data without changing the state of the business data. Example is getStockPrice.

Now armed with this taxonomy of business services, it helps prospective consumers determine where to first look for reusable services. Or the taxonomy helps architects determine the software stack necessary to address qualities of service. The point is that categorization is often advantageous as the label tells the consumer, the practitioner, something about the service like granularity (such as business sub-process service) or provider type (legacy service). A taxonomy and service classification aids in creating governance models, service ownership models, and reuse as the service repository is organized accordingly. This enables faster access to identifying services that can be reused in future development efforts.

25. Who Owns Service Reuse?

Service reuse is an organizational concern, and ownership should not lie with programmers or developers. Reuse or sharing of services is best achieved when it's understood that the reuse goal is to get the business to reuse more and more business functionalities, both vertically and horizontally. This is facilitated when business stakeholders have a responsibility for increasing sharing and working toward a model where the company can build once and reuse. In many cases, this is also supported if business processes, where it makes sense, can be standard across the enterprise. Service reuse is a shared responsibility between business and IT, and enterprise architecture, having a view to both, should be able to understand and facilitate where service reuse makes sense.

The issue of reuse is getting line of business verticals to share and reuse functionality built and maintained by other verticals and standardizing business processes to promote reuse, which is a governance issue. Some organizations may need to use incentives to change behavior and to increase collaboration and sharing to promote or realize reuse. Enterprise architecture teams play a huge role in reuse by providing an enterprise view of reusable business processes, rules, services, and information needs required by lines of business. Enterprise architecture teams can use their existing governance roles to help lines of business understand the enterprise-shared service portfolio and assist projects and lines of business with awareness of reusable services and how to consume.

Organizations should adopt a service reuse strategy. Build once and only once is often a guiding principle for organizations seeking to increase reuse. A service reuse strategy should have specific goals, describe organizational responsibilities, and describe activities and tasks necessary to promote reuse. Service reuse strategies may not be the same as software reuse strategies. For example, a software reuse strategy may focus on designing software assets in a generic fashion that allows their use in various contexts. A service reuse strategy focuses on building services with known consumers or known scenarios for consumption. A service reuse strategy is also focused on business reuse, not just IT reuse of services. Software reuse strategies deal with overhead issues of reuse where the overhead may be so great as to favor duplication over reuse. Services reuse strategies deal with the standardization of business rules, information, and processes using reusable services.

The enterprise architecture team, common services organizations if they exist, and the executive or management team responsible for deciding when to buy, modify, or otherwise invest in new IT solutions have the responsibility for reuse. A reuse strategy should define the roles and responsibilities of each of these constituents in the reuse of services.

26. What Are the Common Organizational Pitfalls When Adopting SOA?

The most common organizational pitfall in adopting SOA is the failure to account for organizational change management. The second most common pitfall is to only partially perform organizational change management. As discussed in this chapter, SOA is a major change for organizations, fraught with obstacles and organizational resistance. Understanding and assessing the culture makes a huge difference to the sustained success of SOA. Everyone may understand the need for organizational change, but months after early successes, the organizational change practices often begin to diminish, communications become infrequent, executive sponsors think that their focus is no longer required, and the change management program loses steam. The partial implementation of change management occurs when one or more aspects of change management are not performed. Whether that be failure to do an assessment of what works and what needs to be improved, a failure to gain consensus from influential stakeholders, or a failure to have measurable goals, all are causes of failure.

Another common pitfall is not looking at the organization knowledge embedded in executives and practitioners who know what works and does not work in their company. Looking at past failures of other good but failed strategies or projects around sharing provides a treasure trove of data on how to avoid such land mines with SOA.

Many organizations underestimate the value of a shared vision and assume that SOA has a common meaning and value proposition. But after hundreds of projects, it is evident that there often is little consensus in organizations as to what SOA is. Documenting an SOA strategy grounded in business needs becomes integral to understanding what changes are needed for breaking down resistance and realizing the benefits of changing approaches and strategies. Lastly, a failure to address governance directly impacts organizational change, because effective SOA governance is required for SOA strategic goals to be achieved.

Organization: Key Concepts

The relationship between business units and IT must evolve if strategic SOA goals are to be achieved. Present approaches, which entrench silos, must give way to approaches that promote sharing. Much of this is addressed with organizational changes as well as changes in applications, governance, architecture, and methods. Business and IT should evolve to a unified state characterized by a highly collaborative, trust- and business-outcome-focused model. No longer is there a labeling such as "she is from IT" or "he is from business"; instead, parties come together for problem solving, bringing both domain and business expertise to the table.

Organizational change management is a necessity for creating an environment for SOA success. Cultural and behavioral issues surrounding the sharing of services, prioritization, funding, and ownership have to be addressed, and consensus must be reached among lines of business. Barriers to SOA adoption can be flattened, but it requires a holistic approach between business and IT. Service reuse is an organizational concern and focus, with the business playing a huge role in the ownership and promotion of service sharing. Failure to include change management as part of an SOA adoption roadmap is the most common pitfall organizations encounter as an impediment to SOA success.

4

Governance

The primary goal of the SOA is to bind the business world with the world of IT in a way that makes both more efficient. SOA is about creating a bridge that facilitates a symbiotic and synergistic relationship between the two that is more power-ful and valuable than anything that we've experienced in the past. It is only partly about that bridge—the technology that binds the two worlds; it is much more so about the results that can be achieved from having that bridge in place.

—William A Brown, et al., in *SOA Governance, Achieving and Sustaining Business and IT Agility*

Governance and SOA are regularly discussed in tandem, and it is rare to find anyone who does not admit to the value of governance when adopting SOA. At the same time, reactions to SOA governance range from yawns, cynicism, to enthusiasm. These various reactions result largely because governance is invisible to some, misunderstood by others, and has reached stages of bureaucracy for others. So, is SOA governance a necessity, waste of time, or somewhere in between? This chapter addresses these and other issues through the following questions:

27. What is SOA governance?

28. How does an organization get started with SOA governance?

29. What is the role of change management?

30. Does implementation of SOA tools and infrastructure equate to SOA governance?

31. Should service development be centralized in service centers?

32. Does SOA require centers of excellence, architecture boards, or design boards?

33. Why do organizations need to focus on SOA governance when there is an effective enterprise architecture activity?

34. Is SOA governance required for SOA projects to be successful?

35. How can you measure whether SOA governance is effective?

36. What is the difference between design-time and runtime governance?

37. What are common pitfalls of SOA governance?

Governance: Q&A

27. *What Is SOA Governance?*

SOA governance extends IT governance with the context of SOA. SOA involves people, process and technology, is cross-functional involving lines of business and IT. SOA governance extends all aspects of governance present in organizations necessary for creating specific outcomes (e.g., faster time to market for new products) using SOA. Governance activities focus on the outcomes an organization desires to effect via SOA adoption. SOA governance shines a light or magnifies those aspects of IT governance that should be enhanced when seeking to achieve one or more benefits from SOA adoption.

Figure 4.1 illustrates this concept by depicting SOA governance and highlighting aspects of IT governance that might need to be addressed post SOA adoption. For example, enterprise architecture might establish IT principles, standards, and a common infrastructure, any or all of which might need changes (optimize) after SOA adoption. Such changes might include standardizing on an enterprise service bus and a registry.

Investment processes for provisioning new applications and the prioritization process for those investments are examples of process changes that might occur upon the adoption of SOA because existing processes would need to accommodate the provisioning and sharing of services, not just applications or systems. The approach currently used by business and IT stakeholders for prioritizing spending for the next calendar year would change as a result of SOA adoption as organizations begin to adopt a shared-services approach in addition to their current practices related to applications.

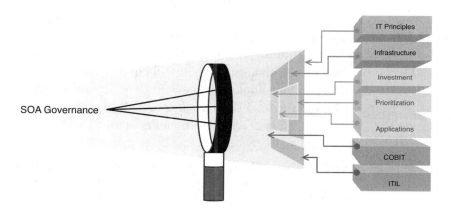

Figure 4.1   SOA governance relationship to IT governance

Organizations that have adopted COBIT (Control Objectives for Information and related Technology), which is an IT governance framework and toolset, or ITIL (Information Technology Infrastructure Library), which is a set of practices for IT service management, might make adjustments to accommodate specific SOA adoption goals in their organization. For example, ITIL provides an excellent list of practices that are largely IT focused. With SOA adoption, it would be useful to have business metrics captured reflecting whether the business process has met key performance indicators, or whether business and IT alignment is progressing according to defined metrics. In this example, the business process metrics and the business/IT alignment, SOA governance activities would surface the ITIL changes to advance SOA adoption.

Numerous studies, books, and articles examine the value of IT governance. Peter Weill and Jeanne W. Ross write in *IT Governance:*

How Top Performers Manage IT Decisions Rights for Superior Results (Harvard Business School Press, 2004) that "effective IT governance is the single most important predictor of value an organization generates from IT." It is also established that top-performing companies, measured by year-to-year profit and revenue growth, succeed where others fail with the effective implementation of IT governance. Anecdotally, everyone knows the effects of excellent IT governance: Projects get completed on time and deliver the desired business results, costs are lower because infrastructure and applications are shared whenever possible, standards are used to drive efficiency, and excellent relationships develop between business and IT groups. Given the breadth of SOA, it only makes sense that establishing effective IT governance in the context of SOA, organizations can see SOA benefits realized. SOA governance is about changing IT governance to make it more effective using the construct of services and SOA benefits as the change agent.

Different types of governance are present in an enterprise, as illustrated in Figure 4.2. Corporate governance establishes the rules and the manner in which an enterprise conducts business based on its strategy, marketplace, and principles. IT governance defines a structure of relationships and processes to direct and control the enterprise in order to achieve the enterprise's goals by adding value while balancing risk versus profit over IT and its processes. SOA governance defines the extensions to IT governance to ensure that the concepts and principles for service orientation and its associated architecture are managed and reused appropriately across the enterprise and the stated business goals for SOA and services are met. SOA governance is often a catalyst for improving IT governance.

SOA governance produces the policies, processes, necessary for controlling development, deployment, and management of services. After a service has been deployed, monitoring and management must be instituted to control and supervise the services eco system. Criteria, processes, and policies need to be constantly checked, communicated, and updated. SOA governance activities focus on the service life cycle from inception of service, to monitoring of the service until the service is retired.

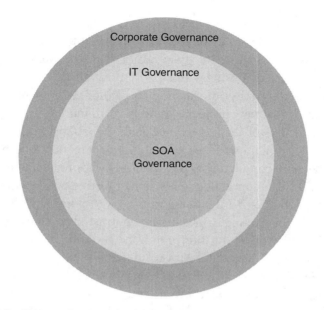

Figure 4.2 Types of enterprise governance

28. How Does an Organization Get Started with SOA Governance?

To initiate SOA governance, an organization must specifically define the SOA goals of the enterprise, line of business, or project. That is, starting SOA governance in a vacuum without the context of goals is possible but often lacks sufficient context to make SOA governance effective. As organizations begin their SOA governance, they must also exercise scope management. After all, organizations don't want to expend undue effort and unnecessary resources to "boil the ocean." Instead, they should "boil a pot of water," define the scope of SOA governance to be commensurate with the context of the initial projects, recognizing that the implementation of SOA governance is gradual and evolutionary.

For example, suppose an SOA initiative is based on these specific goals: increase customer satisfaction, improve time to market, and improve access to information. Suppose further that analysis determined that the existing systems require increased flexibility to realize these goals. Flexibility might be defined as having one interpretation of customer data versus fifty and exposing a "getCustomerVehicleInformation" to dealers, customers, third-party applications and other applications across the enterprise rather than the present situation where each line of business must sort through fifty different data streams to get accurate information. In addition, root cause analysis demonstrates that new projects would have an increasing need to use this discrete unit of business functionality, "getCustomerVehicleInformation." Prior approaches of integration are not as efficient as sharing because connecting applications as an approach means spending time in IT development queues, longer testing cycles and this negatively impacts time to market. Prior to SOA adoption, the current approach of integrating applications, contrasted to sharing services resulted, in fifty different interpretations and integration end points for accessing customer data. As a result of this analysis, a decision to adopt SOA is made and the first SOA project will focus on promoting and using shared services, where shared services can be used by multiple applications now and in the future. This decision to adopt SOA is based on looking at the future portfolio of projects, their prioritization, and a determination that this portfolio will need to share discrete units of business functionality. Sharing the business functionality would improve time to market because the service would be built once and reused; customer satisfaction (e.g., the dealers) would be improved not only because of improved time to market but also because of consistent access to information that they need and use.

Based on this scenario, an organization must answer the four questions shown in Figure 4.3 as they are initiating SOA governance. First, the organization must identify the problem it wants to solve. In our example, the organization wants to create an architecture and environment that promotes the sharing of services for a defined portfolio set. Integrating applications is not as efficient as sharing services. Looking ahead at the queue of enhancements and new requirements, there is a clear need to reuse "getCustomerVehicleInformation." This could be because a new mobile application must be created that needs the service or because a new web based dealer application needs the service. The point is that specific upcoming projects will benefit from using a reusable service, "getCustomerVehicleInformation." The organization knows that integrating applications creates redundancy, longer testing cycles, and often degrades data quality, so an assessment of where they are today has been completed. However, this assessment of their current state shows that the organization must also encourage sharing because there is resistance in the organization as everyone is comfortable with the prior integration approaches and reluctant to take on change as they see it as a risk to project schedules. SOA governance is acknowledged as being needed, helping to answer the third question of where do we need to be tomorrow, and a governance model is defined as part of the target state. The governance model describes the people, process and technology differences from the current state. As part of a planning process the organization decided what if any help is needed to accelerate their goals. Many organizations concentrate their limited SOA talent pool and skills in a center of excellence (CoE) to assist projects, socialize SOA thinking, and develop SOA best practices and assets. The SOA CoE focuses on developing skills with people, on push technology adoption, on extending existing processes, and on promoting shared services.

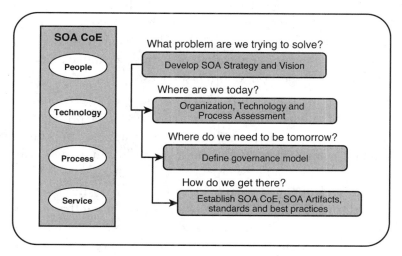

Figure 4.3   How to get started with SOA governance

Getting started with SOA requires a view of where you want to be after SOA adoption is complete. Understanding the problem to be solved defines the scope of SOA governance. The problem could center on cost reduction or time to market savings as examples. However, using the "getCustomerVehicleInformation" example, cost reduction is achieved by not developing the 51st and 52nd integration points for the mobile application or web based dealer application to access customer vehicle information that incur development and maintenance costs. Time to market is faster because new applications can immediately use the deployed "getCustomerVehicleInformation" service without waiting in IT queues for integration. An SOA strategy would codify this and other examples into a statement about the problem being solved and vision for the future. The organization then determines what is working today and where it needs to be tomorrow to make its strategy work. Based on these considerations, the organization can develop a governance model, a model that defines those aspects of IT governance that must be extended to accommodate the SOA principles and goals articulated in the SOA strategy and vision.

In our example, the strategy is focused on identifying and creating a shared service portfolio using an enterprise service bus (ESB) as the primary technology chosen for SOA adoption; approach for removing connectivity logic from applications; allowing applications to focus on business logic; and, allowing each application to change independently. The ESB would make available shared services for use by multiple consumer applications (e.g., mobile application and web-based dealer application) or other services.

The primary message is this: Organizations just getting started with SOA and SOA governance want to focus on specific problems or goals. The integration example was provided because it is a primary motivation for many SOA adoptions and readily illustrates context for how to get started with SOA governance. When looking at SOA value propositions (such as time to market, cost reduction, or flexibility), it helps to perform root cause analysis: What is preventing the realization of the value today? What must be different to realize the value tomorrow? What actions must be undertaken? In most cases, based on this analysis, organizations recognize the need for SOA adoption and the need to improve, extend, or otherwise modify existing IT governance.

Our experience shows that the process of planning (i.e., defining the SOA vision and the problem to be solved), definition (e.g., the scope of SOA governance and metrics), enablement (e.g., establishing a center of excellence, standards and guidelines), and measuring (e.g., assessing metrics and evolving the SOA governance scope) makes SOA governance work most effectively. These four activities (plan, define, enable and measure) are illustrated in Figure 4.4. When performing these four activities issues are uncovered which can be addressed as part of a SOA governance activity. Figure 4.4 lists a representative sample of questions that are typically raised.

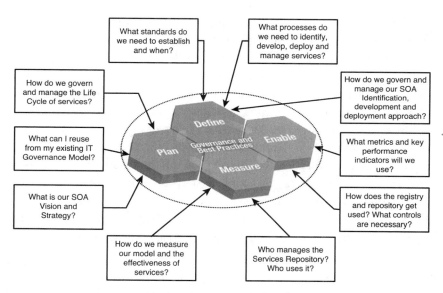

Figure 4.4   Questions for defining the scope of SOA governance

Organizations can develop a laundry list of questions for SOA governance, categorized into buckets of planning, definition, enablement, and measurement. By doing so the scope for SOA governance gets cemented and progress can be plotted against a measurable plan. As a result organizations can avoid the "flexibility bumper stickers" where flexibility is a platitude that appears in strategy documents versus a measurable goal.

29. What Is the Role of Change Management?

Change management is seen from two perspectives in IT. In one perspective, change management is an approach to transform or transition people, groups, or organizations from a current state to a desired future state. In the other perspective, change management is a process whereby changes to a service are formally introduced and approved before deployment into a next testing stage or production state. In the latter case, change management focuses on both changes to a specific version of a service as it progresses through its development life cycle and changes across various versions of a service that must be managed and governed.

The first view of change management defines it as a structured approach for transitioning organizations from a current state to a future state. In this view, the focus is on deciding what if any organizational changes should be made to realize and sustain SOA benefits. Figure 4.5 shows a fairly typical scenario in which organizations start sharing services between lines of business. Everyone agrees that the optimal solution is shared services. However, questions arise concerning who funds the shared service, who owns the shared service, what the responsibilities of a service owner are, and what a service owner is. In some cases, the project stalls as a result of these issues and churn, resulting in missed expectations or project failure. Chapter 3, "Organization," addresses how to use change management to resolve issues on funding and sharing so as to avoid missed opportunities and expectations.

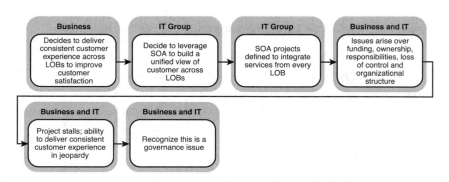

Figure 4.5   Role of change management for SOA governance

Using our example of integration and the ESB implementation in the preceding question, change management is necessary to get lines of business to not only share services but also to share the common infrastructure, the ESB. This results in sustainable cost reduction and promotes sharing of business and technology aspects of

SOA. Change management involves communication, organizational design and change, as well as SOA governance so that executives and managers are aware to what they have committed to in SOA governance. Lack of clarity of roles and responsibilities makes it difficult for leaders to influence and educate their teams. Without visible key stakeholders, support for the adoption of SOA governance will dwindle; and the value propositions for SOA will fail to materialize. Change management is essential for successful and effective SOA governance.

The other perspective of change management focuses on changes to a specific version of a service or changes across versions of services (which must also be governed and managed). IT governance for most organizations addresses versioning of software artifacts and release management. If current practices are deficient, they will also be insufficient for SOA. SOA governance and change management play a role in helping organizations deal with the issues of deprecation and staging of services through test stages and ultimately production deployment. Changes to the service interfaces, service implementation, and service contracts must be governed and managed. The role of change management is closely tied to service versioning and is responsible for managing proposed changes to the service portfolio so that the ripple effect and impact of change is contained and minimized to the extent feasible. Services must not only perform consistent with the service contact; services must also be discoverable, the contract interface understandable, and of course, the service must adhere to a demonstrable and proven set of test cases. The service must be stable.

30. Does Implementation of SOA Tools and Infrastructure Equate to SOA Governance?

The software industry has responded to the need for SOA governance by providing software products that support SOA governance, most notably registries and repositories. Such tools provide information about services—metadata that supports versioning, discovery, and management of services both at design time and runtime. It is a well-established best practice in the industry to establish the processes first and then do tool shopping. Establishing the process first and using it provides organizations an opportunity to see what works, what tweaks are required and where gaps exist. The process definition becomes an input feed in helping to define the tool requirements. Of course, the process and tool feed off each other as the process gets modified to reflect what is possible or optimal to perform using the tool. Tools and technology alone does not equate to establishing SOA governance. SOA governance as described in this chapter requires a range of activities (e.g., organizational change, metrics, updated processes and technology adoption) for SOA governance to be established and effective. Design-time and run-time governance are examples of where both process and tools are required for SOA governance. In both cases, understanding the design-time and run-time life cycle process would benefit the activity of selecting the optimal tools.

Design-time governance entails the activities centered on application development using services. Design-time governance covers the full system development life cycle, including requirements management, architecture, design, development, test, documentation, and production deployment. Design-time governance is necessary because it focuses on making information about a service (service descriptions) available at the right time. Design-time governance addresses change management in the context of versioning and release management.

Runtime governance addresses the execution and operational aspects of a service. Monitor the service in the context of business transactions or business activities so that the business can be informed of bottlenecks or other impacts to key business transactions or activities. Effective runtime governance detects performance bottlenecks (for example, throughput or availability) before they occur. Run time governance may include business activity monitoring so that metrics about the performance of business processes (e.g., it completed successfully in a certain time interval). Run time governance can work with policies. Runtime governance should monitor all aspects of service execution with a transaction or business process context.

Various software products can support and automate aspects of design-time and run-time governance, but the tools or software products alone is not sufficient for governance. The effectiveness of design-time and run-time governance is accomplished by having effective processes, people, and the right tools.

31. Should Service Development Be Centralized in Service Centers?

Some organizations developing services have centralized the service development process by creating service centers or centralized service development groups. Often, this approach is selected as an initial way to leverage a limited talent pool available for service development and to ensure that service development uses a consistent set of standards, tools, or architecture building blocks. Centralized service development can provide superior control and enforcement of SOA standards, but on the downside it can operate as a slow funnel for rapid development of services.

Organizations have at their disposal a variety of organizational structures to support service and application development. Factory models and centralized delivery models can all work successfully, but at the same time project management accountability must be present to minimize finger-pointing when, for example, consumers and providers blame each other for schedule slippage or other delivery issues. Centralized service development often means the service provider role will be centralized and service consumers will provide requirements about their service needs. This scenario can create the undesired effect of waterfall development, where the service consumer requires all requirements be well formed in advance of any service development.

Services that have an enterprise scope are often excellent candidates for centralized service development or service centers. Services that require domain knowledge from a line of business and need to be shared by other lines of business are often good candidates for line-of-business service development versus a centralized model. Determining whether something is an enterprise-level service can often be done by looking at whether the business process spans the enterprise or is specific to a line of business.

Effective SOA governance is a critical success factor when organizations employ factories or services centers for service development. Design authorities can be used to direct the build and construction activities. Using design authorities allows projects to be reviewed for architecture and design compliance, providing the necessary controls for effective SOA governance.

32. Does SOA Require Centers of Excellence, Architecture Boards, or Design Boards?

A successful SOA program that helps transform the enterprise into an agile one with supporting adaptive IT infrastructure requires a combination of enablers. One key enabler is the implementation of governance around SOA. This governance is not achievable without a governing body consisting of respected technical and business leaders within the organization who collaborate to achieve consensus on architectural and design aspects that impact the organization as a whole.

An SOA CoE (Center of Excellence) facilitates the realization of business value through the implementation of SOA and leads corporate-wide business and technical communities in enabling business agility through shared and reusable services. The SOA CoE crosses operational and organizational boundaries to enhance awareness of shared services, operates as a technical aid to projects, provides education and training to projects teams, conducts architecture reviews, promotes asset adoption, resolves technical issues, and provides instructional guidance in the context of active projects on SOA standards and best practices.

An architectural board is often an existing enterprise architecture board or a newly established SOA leadership board that provides visibility and commitment to SOA adoptions. Often, the architecture board performs four governance processes: compliance, exception and appeals, vitality, and communication.

Governance Process	Process Description
Compliance Process	Provides the review, approval, and reject process using criteria agreed upon as part of establishing the governance model.
Exceptions and Appeals Process	Describes the process for allowing appeals and exceptions for non-compliance to standards, architecture, or other guiding principles.
Vitality Process	Process for keeping governance applicable and pertinent to all stakeholders. This process defines the activities that must consistently be performed to sustain a collaborative and healthy governance program.
Communication Process	Defines the process for continuous education, training, and communication of different stakeholders necessary for the sustained success of governance.

Design boards or design authorities may be the same as an architectural board and perform similar functions, or organizations might assign different responsibilities to each. Design authorities participate in quality-assurance reviews for shared services, identify services that can be reused by project teams, and direct project design activities that relate to shared services.

These boards are formal constructs that require participation and support from all business lines. Such boards will require time and patience to become productive as it takes time to mature the relationships and create fruitful consensus-driven collaboration; to agree and adhere to a set of guiding and common principles. Therefore, it is essential to grow boards as organizational capabilities, which in some cases might mean "bootstrapping" or growing gradually with increasing participation and circumference of influence.

Figure 4.6 shows the relationships between various organizational constructs such as design authorities, architecture boards, and CoEs. The SOA CoE works directly with projects to flatten SOA issues and to accelerate adoption of SOA. The SOA CoE may perform a variety of activities to fulfill its mission, which is ultimately to make projects teams more efficient and effective. These activities may be on-the-job training, skills transfer, subject matter expertise, development assistance, or anything required making the project team effective. SOA CoE team members in some organizations will take direction from an architecture board or design authority. The architecture board or design authority provides project direction and may escalate to the SOA leadership board for approval of important decisions. The architecture board or design authority is also responsible for the architecture and establishes architectural direction for SOA to application development teams in the use of architectural frameworks, standards or reference architectures.

The SOA leadership board provides the tactical leadership needed to direct and control SOA activities across the enterprise, which includes establishing SOA governance policies, standards, and processes. This board ensures the vitality of SOA and that necessary communication occurs among all stakeholders across the enterprise. This board tracks and reports against defined metrics to gauge the progress of SOA in achieving its strategic and tactical benefits. An

SOA executive steering committee provides visibility and commitment to SOA within the enterprise and brings proper focus to bear
when necessary to remove political roadblocks or other obstructions.
The SOA executive steering committee also ensures business involve-
ment and commitment to SOA adoption.

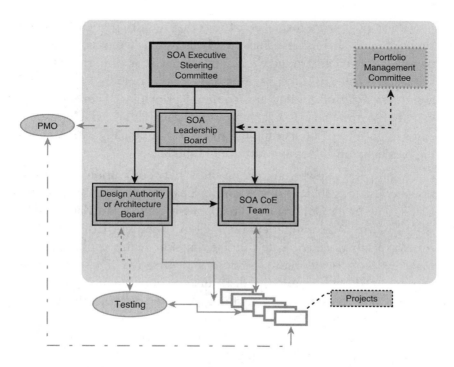

Figure 4.6   SOA CoEs and architecture boards

The project management office (PMO), if necessary and in place,
works with the various committees, boards, and CoE to ensure that
projects are delivered on time, within budget, and consistent with
measurable SOA goals. For example, if flexibility is a business goal, all
parties depicted in Figure 4.6 will work cooperatively to ensure flexibility is not just a platitude but also a measurable feature to be realized in one or more projects. Most organizations have a function
responsible for portfolio management where projects are funded and
prioritized.

33. Why Do Organizations Need to Focus on SOA Governance When There Is an Effective Enterprise Architecture Activity?

SOA requires additions to standard enterprise architecture practices and processes. The notion of a central service model, for example, is unique to SOA; enterprise architecture must adjust to address handling of service models as a vehicle to promote sharing across the enterprise. Governance plays a role in how enterprise architecture (EA) teams augment their current practices to address SOA. Organizations with effective enterprise architecture perform four governance processes and they use these same processes with the adoption of SOA:

- A **vitality process** maintains the applicability and currency of the architecture reflecting the business and IT direction and strategy. Architectural principles are often used to guide the vitality process. SOA adoption adds new architectural principles such as, "Service models will be used to capture the enterprise portfolio of shared services."

- A **compliance process** reviews and approves or rejects the design of a solution. This process can be performed at various points throughout the business and project life cycle. EA teams will review SOA artifacts for compliance to SOA reference architecture or standards as an example.

- A **communication process** educates and communicates the architecture across the organization. This includes ensuring easy access to and consumption of architectural information and assets. Implementing SOA requires communication decks, white papers and training materials be updated to reflect SOA adoption at the enterprise level. This includes standards, architectural guidance, reference architecture and refinements to any architectural building blocks necessary for SOA.

- An **exception and appeals process** allows projects to appeal the noncompliance of a solution or design decision or investment with the board and perhaps be granted an exception. Project teams will need to make architectural decisions that in some cases may conflict with an architectural standard. The EA team will listen and grant exceptions as necessary for projects employing SOA.

SOA governance uses the exact same governance processes found with effective enterprise architecture. Where effective IT governance is in place, SOA governance operates solely to enhance. SOA governance does not introduce any new governance processes; it introduces new processes to be governed, such as service identification, service design, service funding, service domain owners, and service runtime.

The following table reflects the influence EA has on SOA projects at the enterprise and project level using models and guidance. An example of a model at the enterprise scale is an architectural framework that organizes architectural building blocks. Design frameworks for SOA accompanied with code is an example of a model that can be used at the project scale. An example of guidance is a reference architecture that could be used across the enterprise or at the project level providing prescriptive guidance on how to elaborate a solution's SOA.

	Models	Guidance
Enterprise scale, or things which help plan and organize work	Enterprise Models	Architecture building blocks, Usage principles, Reference models
Project scale, or those things focused on building or implementing things	Program and Project Models	

A focus on SOA governance often provides the genesis for updating EA models such as an architectural framework. Figure 4.7 depicts a workflow of various EA activities culminating in using the architecture framework that has been updated to address SOA. The architecture framework can be automated and visually represented where project teams, solution designers, can programmers can find and reuse content. EA architectural frameworks can also be linked to repositories to facilitate locating services at design time.

Figure 4.7 illustrates a workflow where services, design patterns and reference architecture are architectural building blocks reflected in EA model, enterprise architecture framework, an enterprise scale model, to facilitate classification and location of architectural building blocks. In this workflow the EA provides a framework to facilitate reuse, assets to providing project guidance and assets that help in the construction of applications. Solution designers use the architectural framework to accelerate development of applications or services. For many organizations, it will be the output of activities associated with SOA governance that causes the enterprise architecture framework to get updated to reflect SOA building blocks. In some cases, SOA governance will be the genesis for the renewal and a more effective Enterprise Architecture.

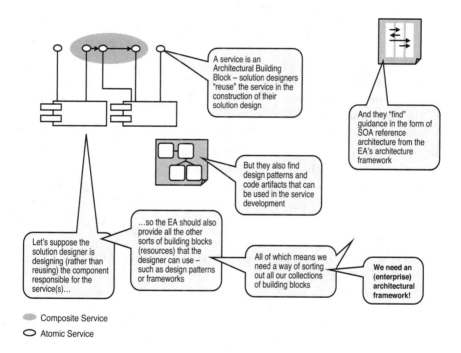

Figure 4.7 Enterprise Architecture framework

34. Is SOA Governance Required for SOA Projects to Be Successful?

Organizations can successfully implement an SOA project without SOA governance; however, the strategic and tactical benefits of SOA, as described in Chapter 2, "Business," cannot be delivered without effective SOA governance. Ensuring that SOA projects produce acceptable results requires key performance indicators or success metrics that provides the expected results from SOA governance. Thus, one of the processes to be governed is the SOA system development process providing guidance on how to identify, design and develop reusable services. Such guidance avoids service proliferation where a lot of services are developed but very few are reusable. SOA governance focuses on people, processes and technology that moved in unison to increase the reuse of services.

When SOA is adopted, we find organizations at different levels of maturity in IT governance and SOA governance. In some cases, this means that each line of business looks after its own interests, and the result can be inefficiency, higher costs, and a viewpoint that it is always cheaper for a line of business to develop something itself rather than reuse a service or infrastructure built by another line of business or organization. Most organizations have good citizens, so often the reason for a lack of commitment, to a shared or centralized strategy is a perception of higher risk (i.e., "do not have control over my destiny because I must rely on other organizations") or its cheaper or faster to do it within the line of business than to work with other lines of business or a centralized team. Effective SOA governance addresses the people, process and technology issues that may prevent achievement of both strategic and tactical goals for SOA adoption.

35. How Can You Measure Whether SOA Governance Is Effective?

SOA governance requires measurements in several areas: business benefits, project costs, and service utilization. Chapter 2 lists potential business benefits and associated metrics that can be tracked to determine whether business benefits are realized from SOA adoption. If a desired business benefit does not accrue in the planned time horizon, it is a sure bet that there is ineffective SOA governance. Effective SOA governance also helps organizations identify the likelihood of a benefit accruing and when.

SOA governance has a number of key processes that should be implemented. One of these is a process that ensures vitality and currency of the SOA governance policies and processes. Metrics are gathered at key points to provide feedback for ascertaining that the governance processes in place are indeed effective. Defining metrics at key stages of the service life cycle and system development life cycle is a most effective way of gauging the effectiveness of SOA governance.

For most organizations, when there is a failure to achieve any of the following, a red flag should be raised as to the effectiveness of SOA governance:

- Reduce the time to deploy business functions or changes to existing functions
- Reuse SOA assets by other projects or lines of business
- Improve flexibility of applications
- Utilize ESB to reduce costs
- Reduce maintenance costs
- Achieve development savings in new development of shared services

36. What Is the Difference Between Design-Time and Runtime Governance?

Design time governance includes the definition of policies and proper life cycle associated with a service as it is designed, tested, implemented, monitored, and registered in the service registry. Design-time governance provides a full life cycle view of a service from inception to deployment to retirement. Design-time governance uses registry and repository tools to track service design, management, policies, and any artifacts associated with the service. Such artifacts might include a test report demonstrating that a service successfully passed certain quality-assurance tests. Design-time governance includes design tools to facilitate the modeling and creation of services, deployment tools addressing service implementation, and test tools.

Runtime governance uses the operational policies to monitor the runtime execution of the services against the policy criteria defined and against operational requirements such as service level agreements. Runtime governance practices address managing the quality of a service such that a service is known in the context of its application flow or business transactions. For example, services from some categories of users may allow a 5-7 second response time but for others it must be 2-3 seconds. Or at a certain time of day, inquiry transactions receive a lower priority than deposit transactions. Service dependencies and consumers, across a heterogeneous environment, are known as part of runtime governance allowing context rich policies to be defined. Metadata is accessible at runtime and describes the expected service availability, throughput, business owner, and any other pertinent information necessary to manage, secure, and operate the service. Security is another aspect of runtime governance where enforcement occurs through authentication, authorization, or credential mapping. Service virtualization to handle load balancing, routing, or failover is another aspect of runtime governance.

37. What Are Common Pitfalls of SOA Governance?

"Trying to do too much too soon" is a common syndrome. "Ironfisted" or heavyweight governance is another common problem. In addition to these two common problems, the following are common pitfalls of SOA governance:

- SOA governance becomes solely about a focus on integration.
- Lines of business resist SOA adoption and avoid sharing services.
- SOA efforts become "shelf ware."
- Funding issues and SOA projects drag to a halt.
- Failure to achieve reuse or time to market savings.
- Toothless governance.
- SOA goals take a backseat to tactical project goals.
- SOA governance is ineffective if poor IT governance prevails.
- Selling SOA versus specific measurable strategic or tactical benefits of adopting SOA.

SOA is more than the sum of the technologies that enable SOA. SOA governance recognizes the synergistic and overlaps between technology, people and processes to achieve strategic SOA goals. SOA governance should have a scope focused on achieving one or more measurable strategic or tactical goals. SOA governance requires active support from senior executives with authority and influence. With large-scale projects, SOA is often a strategic goal with a larger focus on delivering a business solution with its own sets of challenges. Senior executives can ensure that the strategic goals are baked into the project scope. Architects can make sure these goals are measurable and achievable.

Defining value propositions for lines of business to use and share services and SOA assets is something that SOA governance and change management can positively influence. Management support and delegation of the SOA charge to key respected leaders coupled with grassroots building of consensus of the method to gradually deploy governance is essential.

Establishing an SOA funding model for both short- and long-term initiatives is another critical success factor for SOA governance. There must be some commitment to funding dedicated resources necessary for SOA stewardship (e.g., SOA CoE and SOA governance activities) and the procurement of supporting SOA tools (e.g., design time and runtime) and technologies. Funding for SOA projects must be crafted in a manner that advantages and incents lines of business. Establishing incentives that reward lines of business for serving enterprise goals is an example. Governance bootstrapping that starts with a lightweight approach to governance consisting of an architecture review board consisting of key respected leaders from both the business and technical sides is a prudent and effective way to get started.

Governance: Key Concepts

Governance is about establishing chains of responsibility, authority, and communication to empower people (decision rights). Effective governance requires establishing measurements, policy, and control mechanisms to enable people to carry out their roles and responsibilities. Governance determines who is responsible for making the decisions, and management is the process of making and implementing the decisions. SOA governance often entails the reengineering of IT governance as SOA governance shines a light on IT governance, in much the same way that data governance did to IT governance some decades ago. We talk about SOA governance as separate from IT governance not because it is separate but because of the focus on what improvements or changes are required to existing IT governance for SOA benefits to be realized and sustained.

SOA governance is not a one-size-fits-all solution, and the scope of SOA governance and defined metrics are key success factors for effective SOA governance. SOA governance matters if organizations are to realize the business benefits of SOA (e.g., business flexibility and improved time to market savings). SOA governance mitigates business risk, helps maintain the quality of services, and ensures consistency of services. SOA governance also improves team effectiveness as we measure the correct things, and communication between business and IT is improved.

Real-world experience demonstrates that effective governance coupled with a compelling SOA vision and a proactive plan provides big payoffs for organizations. Governance is not just about compliance; it is about promoting the right projects and making them better. With the right focus, support, and funding, SOA governance can be an enabler by facilitating reuse, prioritizing spending, reducing costs, and setting the technology direction. There must be a concerted effort to streamline and empower governance processes wherever possible, giving them teeth and making them efficient. Centers of excellence provide an opportunity to significantly accelerate an organizational path up the SOA learning curve and actually bring the focus to business impact and innovation. SOA CoEs also provide employees with an enabling environment for expanding skills and advancing their careers.

5

Methods

System development is primarily concerned with program-
ming. I will show that a relatively small part of the develop-
ment process is devoted to the coding activity and that most
errors are failures in design and not coding.

Once a program is delivered, the job is finished. A corollary
myth is that maintenance is just fixing errors. I will show that
about two-thirds of the lifetime cost for a system comes after
installation and that only one-fifth of that effort involves error
correction. This, structuring the process to optimize for devel-
opment is shortsighted.

—Bruce I. Blum in *Software Engineering: A Holistic View*

Delivering quality products, keeping up with demand, delivering
to specification, on-budget and on-time delivery—these are a few of
the application management issues organizations face. SOA-based
methods address these issues beyond what non-SOA-based methods
do. SOA-based methods provide relief for these issues by focusing on
the following areas: increasing reuse, improving business and IT collaboration, engineering applications so that they can easily be
changed, and reducing the lifetime costs of an application and
thereby reducing the problem citied by Blum where two-thirds of the
lifetime cost of a system comes after installation. This is why SOA-
based methods matter.

Methods and system development life cycles should adopt SOA
principles, because SOA is another turn of the crank, an evolutionary

improvement in application development methods and system development life cycles. This chapter describes SOA-based methods and how they differ by answering the following questions:

38. Should an organization continue to use agile or object development methods for SOA projects?

39. What changes in system development result from SOA?

40. Does SOA require service modeling?

41. How should services be identified or specified to maximize reuse?

42. How should the granularity of a service be determined?

43. Should SOA be used only for custom development projects?

44. Are any new development roles introduced by SOA methods?

45. Does SOA change testing methods?

46. How do SOA methods accelerate application development?

47. How do SOA methods reduce lifetime costs for applications?

48. What are the common pitfalls in adopting SOA methods?

Methods: Q&A

38. Should an Organization Continue to Use Agile or Object Development Methods for SOA Projects?

Agile methods or object development methods provide insufficient guidance for SOA projects. Agile methods focus on iterative development, allowing requirements and the solution to evolve through collaboration using cross-functional teams, which include business and IT stakeholders. Object methodologies focus on object modeling and object technologies to guide the development of solutions. In both agile and object methods, the focus on service development is absent. Agile and object methods represent best practices in system development methods. However, organizations expecting to achieve the benefits of SOA will need to enhance these methods to include SOA.

Many of the current system development methods focus on making IT more effective, cheaper, or faster, whereas SOA methods focus on making the business and IT more effective and faster. SOA methods provide prescriptive software engineering guidance by addressing the following:

- They provide guidance on how to identify and develop reusable business services that can be reconfigured to provide new business capability or repurposed to serve different business processes or market opportunities.
- They focus on how to reduce, using services, the lifetime cost of the application.
- They reduce system development activities, allowing for an accelerated system development process using services.
- They allow engineer applications to be built for change.

To identify and build reusable, reconfigurable, and flexible services as business assets, you must change existing methods to accommodate the identification, specification, and realization of five primary constructs:

- Business processes
- Services
- Components
- Information
- Rules/policies (and their flows)

A business service catalog will be the result, which will grow over time, project by project. Business services should be reused across applications and channels supporting vertical and horizontal business processes. SOA methods provide guidance on how to identify, specify, and realize reusable business services.

Reducing system development activities and thereby accelerating the system development process requires reducing the aspects of the system development life cycle that are consuming the most calendar time. Most calendar time is consumed with figuring out what to do, the requirements process, and testing cycles. Services will help reduce the calendar time during requirements formation by adding the concept of provisioning and reusing services as part of the requirements life cycle. Reuse no longer becomes an activity the developer or programmer does. Instead, it becomes an activity the business does as part of its deciding to build a new application or change an existing application. Accelerating the testing cycle using services is accomplished as the scope of what needs to be tested is reduced.

39. What Changes in System Development Result from SOA?

A key change introduced in system development and methods because of SOA is service identification (that is, understanding how to identify services that are reusable and fulfill business goals). Service identification is a key activity of building systems using SOA. The conversation between business and IT shifts from conversations that result in functional silos and applications (conversations that focus on functional needs and lists of functional requirements) to a conversation about which services are needed to meet business needs or goals. Although subtle, this change in conversation profoundly impact scope management and requirement prioritization.

Scope management changes from managing a large set of functional requirements to managing a smaller set of prioritized services. Services are prioritized based on how they satisfy business goals, based on the importance of the business goal or the number of business goals fulfilled. This forces a conversation with the business—not about every feature, but about whether a coarse-grained piece of business functionality, a service, is needed in the next release or a future release.

In addition to the changes and improvement in scope and requirements management, the SOA approach of service identification has other advantages. One advantage is the early look for reuse, determining whether the service exists and can be reused. It's not about programmers trying to reuse things; it's about the business reusing things. Instead of a laundry list of functional requirements or use cases that need to be prioritized, these lists are replaced with a service portfolio, which is a categorized and rationalized set of business capabilities that fulfill specific business goals. The thinking shifts to understanding that services have the highest priority. The conversation differs dramatically because any service we want to create or enhance must be tied to one or more business goals. Instead of a large and perhaps complex set of requirements that must be examined, understood, and prioritized, we have a set of candidate services that can be easily understood and prioritized.

Figure 5.1 provides an example of a goal service model. The figure shows three specified goals, and each goal has a key performance indicator, making each goal measurable. The list of services is also provided, and each service fulfills one or more of the documented business goals. The services can be prioritized based on how many of the goals are fulfilled.

Goal	Key Performance Indicator
1. Increase the speed and agility in delivering new business services	Time to deliver a new business service is 2 weeks
2. Streamline processes to reduce operating costs	Operating cost reduction reduced by 20% after system deployment
3. Increase revenue by 20% by the end of next year	Revenue increase year to year by 20%

Business Service	Goal Satisfied
Maintain Customer Relationships	1, 2, and 3
Manage Customer Service Claim	1, 3
Perform Customer Notification	2

Figure 5.1   Example of a goal service model

The effect of this change is that using services breaks down functional silos, where instead of locking business capability in applications, function is segmented into functional boundaries, services. Using services in this manner creates a way to structure the application around services versus objects or components. In the former, the service is instantiated with components but the service has a life cycle similar to an application has a life cycle, enabling the services to be deployed independently of other services and tested independently. The service life cycle improves impact analysis when making changes because changes are functionally isolated in services versus spread over a large code base of components, objects, or modules. Test cycles are reduced when introducing a service life cycle because only modified services need to be included in a test cycle. Reducing impact analysis and reducing testing cycles contributes to a less-brittle application and a lower lifetime cost of the application. Applications engineered in this fashion are built to change, and applications built to change provide agility.

A second change in system development as a result of SOA is brought about by adapting methods to include guidance on granularity: how big or small should a service be to maximize reuse. Other factors that influence the granularity include the usage scenario for the service, consumers, business process flexibility, enterprise/partner integration, and quality of service attributes.

Service specification is the third change in system development resulting from SOA. The specification of the service, its dependencies on other services, the service contract, and business alignment facilitate the design and build of the components that realize the service. Service specification aids in creating atomic services so that each service can participate in its own service life cycle, much the same way as applications participate in their own life cycle from ideation to deployment to retirement. Defending against service proliferation is also addressed by SOA-based methods because the method focuses on service reuse.

One last change brought about using SOA methods centers on artifacts. SOA methods introduce a new artifact, a service model and its relationship to a widely used existing artifact, a use case model. A service model is used to capture the service portfolio, the list of services, a description of the service, and dependencies on other services. Another artifact already in place for many organizations in system development is a use case. Use cases capture functional requirements that describe a system's behavioral requirement by describing scenarios. System development changes as a service model should be created, and the service model should precede the development of use cases. The use cases can then be used to describe the functional requirements for the identified services. This change, whereby you develop the service model and then the use case model, versus identifying services from the use case model, makes a big difference in breaking down application silos and creating reusable services. Services developed in this manner, being supported with their own use cases, are more loosely coupled and insulated from other services, with each service having a clearly defined purpose.

40. Does SOA Require Service Modeling?

Because SOA projects vary in size and scope, not all SOA projects require service modeling. SOA projects whose goals include engineering business applications that are built to change, leveraging and reusing business services, reducing the lifetime costs of an application, or using SOA to accelerate time to value require the identification, specification, and realization of services. These SOA projects require service modeling.

The evolution of modeling has passed through various eras, including structured analysis and design, which introduced the dichotomies of data-centered and process-centered modeling. Later, object modeling was introduced as a method to develop object-oriented systems. Component-based software engineering then advanced the state of the art and built on the foundation laid by object orientation by introducing component modeling. Service modeling advances the state of the art further.

Dealing with services as first-class constructs, on par with applications as business assets, requires more than traditional object-oriented or component-based paradigms. Elevation of the notion of programming to interfaces rather than implementations into an architectural construct of a layer in the architecture was a bold step in the evolution of software engineering. The service interface and the service contract are key elements to identify, specify, realize, and implement services. SOA augments methods by adding service modeling. The change from current modeling approaches to service modeling can be seen on a spectrum: from those who advocate that "only the packaging is new" to those who believe a new paradigm exists.

Modeling is seen in every human endeavor because models enable people to deal with complexity. Modeling helps solve problems by representing complex things at a higher level of abstraction. SOA is another opportunity to raise the level of abstraction by decoupling the provider of the service from the consumer of the service, where the service model identifies the business processes that consume services or identifies the services and the components that realize the business functionality.

Service modeling focuses on the set of business capabilities and related IT functionality as a set of services, the components that implement them, and the processes that invoke them or string the services together into a composite service or application, as illustrated in Figure 5.2. Service modeling should be holistic and address the modeling of activities or flows, services, and their components. The modeling is iterative and business centric. Figure 5.2 illustrates the scope of service modeling using business processes as a source for service identification. Services and their relationships with other services are defined during the modeling exercise along with the necessary components. A service needs to be modeled from business and runtime perspectives such that the service fulfills a key step or activity of a business process, is shareable and reusable, and meets the expected quality of service attributes at runtime.

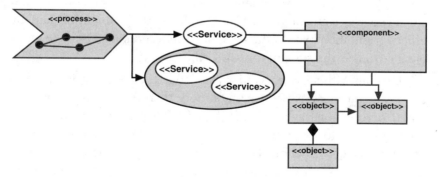

Figure 5.2   Elements of service modeling

Service modeling produces a categorized list of services, business functionality, and capabilities required by the business. This list can be described as a service portfolio. Because a service portfolio provides a list of assets that the business can leverage and reuse, it can be used by any project . Extending methods to provide service modeling represents a best practice of software and systems engineering.

A negative consequence of not performing service modeling is that application architectures will be structured in much the same way they are today, using current system development approaches and resulting in the same problems plaguing the business and IT: application silos, increasing costs of maintenance, business processes difficult to change, and IT systems constraining business flexibility. No service modeling often means a plethora of services (service proliferation), which creates a large mass of increasingly unmanageable services that often require ongoing rationalization and refactoring, thus increasing total cost of ownership.

41. How Should Services Be Identified or Specified to Maximize Reuse?

A key tenet of understanding SOA is the focus on getting the organization to reuse versus a focus on the programmer to reuse. Robert L. Glass, software engineer, professor, and author, wrote in his book, *Facts and Fallacies of Software Engineering,* that reuse in coarse-grained or large components remains mostly an unsolved problem even though everyone agrees it's important and desirable. The problem, he asserts, is that when reusable modules are built, they then have to do something that matches a large set of needs in a wide variety of programs. Robert's articles on reuse state that minimal reuse exists because simply not that many software components can be reused. This is why the focus should be on what can be reused at the business or organizational level.

Getting an organization to reuse translates to sharing business functionality across processes or workflows, within the enterprise and with partners. It requires that sharable functionality be engineered in a manner that allows sharing: Build once and share regardless of the consumer platform. This engineering requires the identification and realization of services. The identification phase in an SOA project includes not just the identification of services, but also the identification of processes, information, rules, and components. Our experience indicates that it is a best practice to utilize a set of complementary service identification techniques. Relying on a single technique tends to create either an incomplete set of services or services without the necessary granularity to effectuate reuse and flexibility. A single technique often introduces information entropy early in the development life cycle, often to be remedied at greater cost later in the service life cycle because it entails greater efforts of service refactoring to eliminate redundancies or make the service coarser for higher business value. In addition, this often leads to the failure to identify service dependencies early on, which impacts release planning and, ultimately, project delivery.

When designing a service portfolio, you should use a combination of service identification techniques to cast a more complete net and catch the necessary services required to support a business. Some projects might choose to lead with information, whereas others choose a business process focus. Each of the techniques can be used to start the process of service identification and then use the subsequent ones to work in concert from different angles: process, information, top down, bottom up, exploring the commonality and variations across processes, information, rules, policies, and events. Any technique that is not applicable or of little value on a given project should be omitted or its usage minimized.

Services are optimally identified using three complementary techniques that provide a balance between tactical imperatives and strategic vision:

- **Goal service modeling** looks at business opportunities, strategy, and business goals to both confirm and validate that candidate services have been identified, which fulfill goals and enable the business strategy.

- **Domain decomposition** focuses on business process modeling, rules, information, and potential variability of services.

- **Asset analysis** addresses the reality that businesses have accumulated legacy systems and applications that must be integrated, enhanced, or leveraged. This bottom-up approach looks at the existing application portfolio and other assets that can be used in identifying candidates for service exposure. In contrast, goal service modeling combines the top-down (domain decomposition) and bottom-up (asset analysis) approaches and pulls them together into alignment.

Building and sharing common services that can be leveraged across multiple lines of business or the enterprise requires leveraging and reusing assets, services. The failure to share services and repurpose them in new ways puts an organization in the situation of re-creating something that has been done 60% to 100% the same way, and development dollars are spent needlessly re-creating functionality that already lives in the application portfolio of the enterprise. Sharing services does require change management and governance, which are addressed in Chapter 3, "Organization," and Chapter 4, "Governance." Sharing services requires that you identify and build the right services, which are what the three complementary techniques of service identification promote.

Instead of focusing on common services, the focus is on shared business processes and standard business processes. In turn, having shared services, multipurpose, multiconsumer services sourced from business processes, existing assets, information, and business goals affords the best opportunity to identify and build the right services that are shareable. Trying to identify common services should not be the goal. Instead, the goal should be on the identification and build out of services based on business goals and business processes using the three complementary techniques that result in the desired effect and shared and common services.

The services to provide or consume can be summarized and centralized in a service model. The service model includes a categorized list of services called the service portfolio. These services are abstracted into a layer in the architecture that decouples providers and consumers, through a service contract. The service model becomes an essential asset to promote reuse, which can be automated using a registry for search, dynamic binding, versioning, and other full life cycle governance features that facilitate reuse.

Using standard business processes and eliminating duplicate business processes can make a big difference in enabling sharing of processes. This is a primary reason business processes must be visible, understood, consolidated, and maintained for the life of the system, as a way for IT to maintain its connection to the business to continue to represent and understand evolving business needs.

Use cases have been widely used and recognized as a best practice for the capture of functional requirements. A use case captures a set of static actor-object interactions that ultimately realize the use case. These flows are most often invariable and hard-coded. This does not allow the easy recombination of functionality. Variability affects reuse and sharable services because these seemingly infinitesimal differences lie at the heart of the lack of reuse.

In contrast, in variation-oriented analysis, a service case identifies the reconfigurable choreography of a set of service operations, each a unit of functionality. This flow is not hard-coded. Instead of endeavoring to initially identify the objects that sequence the interactions, the focus is on the set of business aligned services that collectively enable the fulfillment of business goals, and the services can be recombined in unanticipated service contexts. Rather than being just an actor interacting with a system, the service is part of an ecosystem of providers and consumers with often interchangeable roles that leverage the services through policies and new combinations in ever-changing use cases.

42. How Should the Granularity of a Service Be Determined?

Granularity speaks to how fine-grained (small units of business functionality) or coarse-grained (large units of business functionality) a service should be engineered to solve a business need. The right granularity depends on context. Most business applications have both fine-grained and coarse-grained services in the service portfolio. Let's look at the pros and cons of each.

Fine-grained services can cause frequent network hops, and thus overhead and inefficiency in their invocation. Coarse-grained services have less network chatter, but are rarely at the right level of detail required. They therefore have a more limited potential for reuse. A service can be modeled so that it can be understood whether a service is too fine because the number of network trips to fulfill an activity of business process is so high it makes the performance of the business process unacceptable. A service can also be modeled so that you can look at a service and determine whether it is too coarse because the ability to make changes independent from the consumers is limited. This reinforces the position that *granularity* is more of an adjective of how a service is described versus a verb and something to do to a service. Granularity is often a focus because of the need to optimize reuse and performance of the service.

The proper granularity of a service or a right service or the optimal service is not about deciding on granularity but on identifying services. If the focus is on service identification, granularity takes care of itself. So, the focus is not on the service, but on the business processes and how the service might meet the needs of multiple business processes and multiple consumers in the enterprise or line of business. The more the service can be leveraged, the more the service fulfills a key step of a business activity, the more the service helps to eliminate redundancy versus promote redundancy, and the more certain we can be that we have the proper granularity. Granularity of a service is driven by the needs of the known and anticipated consumers of the service rather than a design issue that can be determined without the proper context.

43. *Should SOA Be Used Only for Custom Development Projects?*

SOA is useful and recommended for multiple development styles, not only the custom development projects. SOA can be used for several project styles, such as transformation, legacy enhancement, packaged implementation/integration, and information-based projects. Adopting SOA methods does not translate to using web services or exposing services as web services. Adopting service modeling as a basis for structuring applications has multiple advantages regardless of project type:

- **Transformation projects** have goals that cannot be realized by a single project but require a program of projects. Such programs require a vision (an end state or strategy that can be fulfilled). For many organizations, SOA provides a key part of the strategy. SOA becomes the blueprint, starting with a documented vision of the end state using SOA principles and tenets. Companies looking for an application architecture or strategy for transformation consistently adopt SOA.

- **Legacy enhancement** and **legacy transformation** are synonymous terms used to describe the leveraging of existing applications and modernizing them to support new requirements. Legacy enhancement takes on many flavors, and for a lot of companies, this means taking existing application programming interfaces and converting these to service contracts or taking existing systems and wrapping then with web services. Each approach has its advantages and disadvantages, but by applying SOA and services you can extend the life of legacy systems. SOA extends the life of legacy in two ways. The primary way is the avoidance of new legacy systems. The other is using services as façades to enable access to existing legacy business functionality by new channels (e.g., mobile devices), other applications, or external partners.

- **Packaged implementation** often requires extensive integration, so SOA becomes an adoption scenario for both packaged implementations and integration projects. Proliferation of point-to-point solutions is costly to implement and change. Services can be used to integrate packages or integrate disparate systems. An *enterprise service bus* (ESB) is often installed to operate as an intermediary between systems. Services running on the ESB can be deployed and perform routing, protocol conversion, or data transformation. The ESB is the primary adoption pattern for packaged implementation projects. In addition, some companies choose not to adopt or allow the package and its implementation to drive its enterprise or line-of-business data model. That is, some organizations will have their own enterprise data model and packages (e.g., SAP) that are adopted will integrate with existing data models and not supersede the enterprise data model. The service becomes a means to integrate packages with existing systems, using information services, where the enterprise data model is separate and distinct from the data model that comes with the packaged application.

- **Information-based projects** are projects that require aggregation of data into information from many sources, and in which services become the mechanism for both aggregation and integration. For example, in a data warehousing or information analytics solution, services can be used as a means for providing aggregated information from multiple data sources.

44. Are Any New Development Roles Introduced by SOA Methods?

The service architect role emerges as a specialization of the IT architect. The service architect is an IT architect with a focus on service modeling and reuse. The service architect works at both the enterprise and project level to facilitate service reuse. The service architect also creates and promotes service standards that facilitate their usage.

The business stakeholders play a more significant and central role within SOA projects. Business and IT collaboration improves, and instead of functional requirements being defined and sorted into applications, business processes and services are modeled jointly with business and IT stakeholders. Instead of locking business functionality into application towers, business functionality is fulfilled by one or more business services. This process of having the business analyst and service architect work together is sometimes referred to as *two in a box*.

The overlap between business and IT increases as they collaborate, determining what services to provision and when. Figure 5.3 contrasts traditional development and SOA development. As you can see, there is increasing overlap between business and IT stakeholders as they embrace SOA. In SOA development, there is a requirement that business and IT work together to understand business processes, business services, rules, and information needs. Business takes a role in the stewardship of services in areas of ownership and funding. Figure 5.3 depicts the extensive overlap with service orientation, the role of business to model and maintain business process models, and the combined role of business and IT in identifying services.

The service registrar role is new, and this role is responsible for asset repositories with service-appropriate metadata and search capabilities. They also help create and assist with enforcing the organizational discipline necessary for populating the repository. Service registrars discourage the creation of redundant services by making it easy for project teams to scan the repository before beginning design/development efforts on a new service.

SOA boards might be necessary, consisting of line-of-business and IT management. The board is responsible for prioritization of projects and service requests. SOA boards may help with funding for services and may address the issue of funding of shared services. The SOA board has first-line responsibility for review/approval of requests that do and do not meet standards, yet surpass the SOA architecture review team's authority for approval. Based on the governance roles, this function could be performed by an IT steering committee.

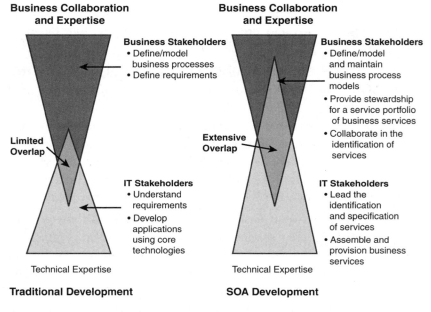

Figure 5.3   Traditional versus service-oriented development

45. Does SOA Change Testing Methods?

SOA methods augment testing methods. The adoption of SOA for agility, reducing lifetime cost of an application or accelerating time to market for new business features, does require a change in current testing methods. These changes will reduce the amount of time it takes to test, enabling you to move faster through test cycles, and will require new activities (e.g., automated regression testing).

Complete testing of all possible paths of a software program, an application, or system has become impractical if not cost-prohibitive for organizations (and has been for some time). There are just too many paths through a program to test; for example, a 100-line program might have 10 to the 8th unique paths. Yet, software defects exist, and organizations must do intelligent testing and full life cycle testing such that defects are identified. For many test teams or test groups, deploying business applications into production with defects is way of life, where defects are now categorized and workaround techniques are communicated in lieu of fixing the defects. It does not have to be this way.

SOA provides an opportunity to improve testing when using services. The use of services promotes black-box testing, where functional tests can focus on valid inputs and outputs. The service contract defines valid inputs and expected outputs of a service, which promotes the use of black-box testing and tools to test the service. Black-box testing eliminates the need to perform complete testing of all possible paths of a program, application, or system.

In most environments, testing of a changed or newly deployed application requires retesting of components in the new system and their connections to downstream systems. This testing cycle is fraught with errors. Often, it must be performed in a linear fashion, and calendar time is slowly eaten away, causing a decision to either delay deployment, turn off features, or simply to live with defects in a production system (where operator workarounds replace functioning software). SOA fixes this issue because a deployed and working service does not need to be retested or included in future test cycles when reusing the service and deploying a new applications that uses the production-deployed service.

Figure 5.4 shows the difference of scope with business applications before and after adopting SOA. In Figure 5.4, the scope of what needs to be tested is larger before SOA. The scope of the test cycle is less with the use of services when a service life cycle is introduced, where each service goes through a testing cycle in the same manner as we treat applications. Just like applications, services do not have to be retested after they are deployed into production. Services can be certified as satisfying their contract specifications. This certification provides consumers confidence that the service works as designed and results in less overall testing when applications are structured using services.

With SOA adoption, where services are the structuring element of the application, black-box testing becomes the norm. This avoids the retesting of services already deployed in production to determine whether the new system, application, or service has a bug, because services working in production continue to accept the proper inputs and deliver the correct outputs according to the service contract.

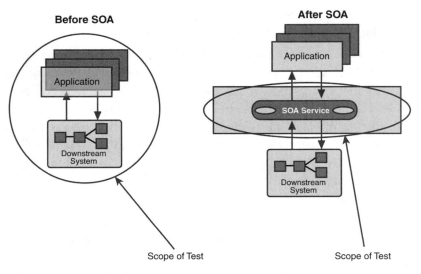

Figure 5.4   SOA and testing

SOA testing is facilitated when automated regression testing is used. Regression testing facilitates the rapid testing of services as black boxes to ensure the service contracts and services work as planned. Test drivers also prove useful for enabling the consumer to test the provider service in a controlled environment and without always having the platform of the service provider available. Service virtualization testing products enable test teams to mimic the functionality of a service based on its contract design before the implementation is developed, which further improves the quality of the service.

46. How Do SOA Methods Accelerate Application Development?

If we look at time to value in terms of faster system development or faster time to market for new functions, SOA methods facilitate these goals using shared services. By focusing on a reusable service portfolio of business capabilities, we have the opportunity to elevate these capabilities as an enterprise asset that is financed, governed, and managed. Having this portfolio, along with the process of periodically refactoring and rationalizing this portfolio, enables organizations to capitalize on shared services. Applications are built through the use of services, also called *assembly*. Assembly is faster than writing code from scratch. Services also enable independent development streams, thus increasing the amount of parallel work that can be concurrently performed, another factor in faster development.

Looking at application development as a process, there are five basic activities: requirements, architecture, construction, testing, and deployment. Accelerating development requires shortening one or more of these process activities. Requirements are accelerated by adopting a reuse approach to thinking about what is needed. Most projects spend quite a bit of calendar time trying to figure out what is needed. With services there is a starting point of a services portfolio. So the goal is to build once and reuse, which is easier to accommodate with services because they lend themselves to reuse more than a coarse grained application. Using services as the starting point rather than a functional list of requirements provides greater focus and structure for scope management, which accelerates the requirements gathering activity; that is, when business stakeholders discuss requirements in the form of services (e.g., we need a create purchase order and invoice purchase order service) versus functional list (e.g., handle purchase orders and provide a purchase order system) it provides improved clarity on functional needs.

Architecture is accelerated as an activity by reusing existing SOA infrastructure for integration. Integration is reduced by adopting and leveraging services and enterprise service buses. Testing is reduced because deployed services do not require re-testing during any testing cycle, thereby reducing the overall test cycle. Services already deployed into production don't require additional implementation activities, as they can be used as-is. Testing is one of the most time-consuming activities in application development, and the adoption of services reduces this activity as the reuse of services increases.

47. How Do SOA Methods Reduce the Lifetime Costs for Applications?

When you are trying to understand how to lower the lifetime cost of an application, it helps to understand the issue raised by Blum. In 1992, Blum stated that two-thirds of the lifetime cost for a system comes after installation and only one-fifth of that effort involves fixing defects. A major reason for two-thirds cost, post deployment of the application, is because applications grow brittle within three to five years of their initial deployment. *Brittle* is defined as an application code base that is difficult to change, expensive to modify, and often results in increasing number of defects as change is introduced. The code base grows more brittle as entropy sets in with time as more changes are applied. Often, the code base gets increasing convoluted (i.e., spaghetti code) as more developers modify the code base, as more code gets copied and pasted as the most tactical method of reuse, and as finding the correct place in the code to make a change becomes increasingly difficult. As a result of these practices, impact analysis to determine where a change should be applied is often incorrect. Changes are not applied to all necessary parts of the code base, and discovery of this defect occurs during testing (or worse, by users in production).

Reducing the lifetime cost of applications necessitates that applications be engineered in a manner that does not cause them to become brittle three to five years after they are first installed into production. SOA methods focus on organizing the application into a set of services. Applications can be traditional or composite applications. In the former, only subsets of the portfolio are services in the latter; the entire building blocks of the application are composed of underlying sets of services. When services are the structuring element, the lifetime cost of the application can be reduced because substantially less effort is involved to change the existing code base when new requirements must be fulfilled. That is, an application structured with services has less spaghetti code, less dead code, less redundant code; and, is organized along functional boundaries, making it easier and faster to identify where to make changes or when to add new services. This has a positive impact on the lifetime cost of the application because the architectural and functional boundaries of the application (loose coupling, cohesion, and separation of concerns) are accomplished and enforced using services.

When the cost in time of testing is added to the discussion, further savings in time to value are achieved because the overall test cycle is reduced because the scope of what has to be tested is less. This reduces calendar time because the test cycle takes less time to complete. Reducing calendar time also reduces cost because fewer people are needed for testing and the resources can be applied to other activities. The net effect of reduced testing is cost savings and time savings.

In summary, when services are used, the potential is significant for substantial improvement in the application architecture and engineering of the application for easy change. If a new business model emerges or new business functionality is required, the cost of this change is limited to the change requested; that is, new requirements do not force a total rework to accommodate them. Services are modified to add new functionality, retired as the business model warrants, or new services are added to the service portfolio.

48. What Are the Common Pitfalls in Adopting SOA Methods?

A common pitfall is to not adopt SOA methods, but (but instead use object-oriented or component-based methods to identify services and) still expect to achieve the benefits of agility and faster time to market that results from true SOA adoption. In such cases, organizations don't realize accelerated system development and ultimately find that they are not receiving any of the desired benefits (reduced cost, agility, or speed to market) from their new functions. This pitfall mostly occurs when SOA is considered as just an architecture tenet or when SOA is seen as related to exposing web services.

A second pitfall is keeping the method only at a project level, even after it has proven to work on a pilot project. Elevating the method to an enterprise level is essential to combining it with governance and providing it at both the enterprise architecture and solution architecture levels. Organizations need to gradually build trust and use common methods that encourage the use of services and sharing of services.

Another pitfall is to fail to leverage expertise (practitioners who have done it before) or fail to use competency centers or centers of excellence to jump-start teams in their SOA adoption. A best practice is to engage practitioners who have successfully completed this initial step many times before. After all, experience and organizational adoption and transformation role models are often key success factors.

A low maturity with agile or iterative methods might impede the adoption of SOA methods, but you can manage such by using outside expertise through centers of excellence. The same applies to modeling when that discipline requires maturation in an organization. Techniques exist for making a method standard even though its implementation might use different development tools.

Of course, the primary pitfall is failure to adopt SOA methods at all. As mentioned previously, SOA method adoption can result in the following benefits (and as a counterpart, no benefits when the SOA methods are not adopted):

- Access any application, function, or data at any time using services
- Leverage reusable services in any context the business desires
- Reduce the lifetime cost of the application portfolio
- Accelerate system development

Methods: Key Concepts

SOA methods should be based on agile, iterative, and collaborative approaches. A low maturity with agile or iterative development can impede successful adoption of SOA methods. Organizations with poor track records in model-based development or modeling may also struggle with the adoption of SOA methods. Standardizing a method can be difficult in a heterogeneous development environment because the tooling (e.g., Rational System Architect versus Visual Studio).

SOA methods differ from other, traditional methods in that SOA treats application resources as services that provide discrete business capabilities, with each service having a well-defined purpose. SOA methods provide guidance on how to structure applications using services. Services become a primary concern in system development and are used to enforce separation of concerns along functional and physical boundaries. Services will also influence a change in testing; the scope of the test gets reduced, and this accelerates system development. Many of the benefits of SOA (e.g., agility, reduced costs, and reuse) can be achieved by adopting SOA methods.

SOA methods are a software process, which is a problem solving activity. The process begins with the identification of a need and culminates with the implementation of a solution that satisfies that need. However, with SOA the need goes beyond simply satisfying functional business needs as organizations adopting SOA have strategic needs that must also be satisfied. These strategic needs have been discussed in the previous chapters such as lowering lifetime cost of applications, building applications that are easy to change or making applications, assets for the business that can easily accommodate new business models or market conditions. SOA methods change how systems and solutions are built to accommodate both the strategic and tactical needs businesses and organizations have for business applications.

6

Applications

Modern corporations are faced with a profound dilemma. Increasingly, they are becoming information-based organizations, dependent on a continuous flow of data for virtually every aspect of their operations. Yet their ability to handle that data is breaking down because the volume of information is expanding faster than the capacity to process it. The result: Corporations are drowning in their own data.

The problem doesn't lie in hardware—computers continue to increase in speed and power at a phenomenal rate. The failure lies in software. Developing software to tap the potential of computers turns out to be a far greater challenge than building faster machines.

—David A. Taylor, Ph.D., in *Object Technology: A Manager's Guide*

Software development is an evolution from art to science—that is, the engineering aspects have improved significantly over the past decades, but as with many human endeavors, some art is mixed with the engineering (or science) regardless of whether we are constructing buildings or bridges or writing software.

We have seen an evolution of engineering improvements that include programming languages, development platforms, database technology, transaction processing, commerce, and the Internet. Yet, the pace of developing software has not kept up with the demands of businesses for rapidly changing business processes and the need for new capabilities. At the heart of this challenge are the applications, whether they are as simple as a spreadsheet used by knowledge workers at their desktops or as robust as a reservation system used by thousands of employees distributed across the world. IT organizations are under tremendous pressure to deliver results with an ever-increasing demand to support a growing set of business-critical needs.

Which applications (or types of applications) that should adopt SOA is relevant, especially when top on the agenda is whether SOA adoption makes applications more responsive to the needs of the business. This chapter addresses questions about applications and SOA with a focus on why SOA matters for applications development and management:

49. Do applications still exist with SOA?

50. Do applications get replaced with composite services/ applications?

51. Is a certain type of business problem best suited for SOA adoption?

52. Is a certain type of IT problem best suited for SOA adoption?

53. What changes with application development when SOA is introduced?

54. What is the relationship of business process management to an application?

55. How does SOA make applications or a portfolio of applications more flexible?

56. Should an application portfolio be managed differently because of SOA adoption?

57. Can existing systems or legacy applications be leveraged when adopting SOA?

58. How are services built that deploy in a cloud?

59. Does it make sense to adopt SOA for one application versus the enterprise?

60. What are common pitfalls for application teams adopting SOA?

Applications: Q&A

49. Do Applications Still Exist with SOA?

Applications continue to exist with SOA. The fundamental building blocks, out of which they are composed, evolve over time. Applications will be constructed out of a combination of services, existing systems, or packaged applications. Applications can be assembled by combining multiple existing functions to create a new application, and this is often described as a composite application; but, it's an application nonetheless. It's the old adage "what's in a name," and whether we call applications composite or not, they are still applications. It is not likely that we will see a large part of portfolios become composite applications simply because of the sheer size of existing application portfolios in most companies and because SOA should not be applied to every application development project.

Applications will be constructed out of orchestrated services, which most likely will adopt business process management (BPM) software to coordinate the orchestration and workflow. Applications constructed using BPM software may comprise (1) services (e.g., Web services invoked by the BPM software as part of the workflow); (2) rules that might be housed in a rules engine; and, (3) control and flow business logic that is part of the process and coded or rendered using BPM software. This will be explained further when we address the question on BPM and its relationship to SOA later in this chapter.

50. Do Applications Get Replaced with Composite Services/Applications?

Composite services are not applications but services that invoke other services. The invocation is independent and without knowledge by the consumer that other services are being invoked. Figure 6.1 illustrates a composite service, Order. Consumers can invoke the Order service by doing a purchaseRequest or a cancelOrder. Creating a purchase order requires two systems: one that provides a material

receipt and another that provides an invoice. When it creates a purchase order (PO), the Order service uses two services: createPurchase to access a legacy CRM application, and a createPurchase for
the legacy ERP system. The Order service manages all interactions
with the two legacy systems, CRM and ERP. It performs two invocations and assembles the multiple responses into one—sending back
to the consumer a single response of an order or cancel depending on
the request. At some future time when redundancy or overlap
between the two legacy systems is resolved and one is retired, it has
no effect on the consuming application since it only knows of the one
service, Order. This improves flexibility for the application portfolio,
as parts can be replaced without impacting the consuming applications. Flexibility is further enhanced as purchase and cancel can be
invoked as Web services, allowing multi-channel access and from
many different types of consumers: mobile applications or web-based
applications.

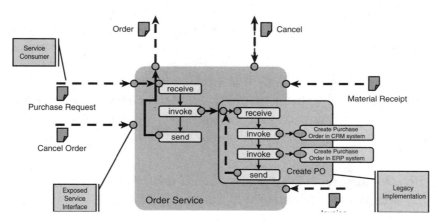

Figure 6.1   Composite service

Composite applications as a term is often associated with SOA,
but composite applications exist independently of adopting SOA, evi-
denced by mashups. Mashups use data or functions from multiple
sources to create a new function. Mashups often use published interfaces (APIs) and data sources to provide new capability. Examples are
public facing solutions that allow government agencies to share information using maps for citizens to discover information on public

safety, schools, obtain permits, or find where to get flu shots. Using local agency data, the web, GPS location services, and map-based solutions, a composite-based application, a mashup, is created allowing faster and more efficient access to government resources and services. Composite applications, and especially mashups, offer another way to deliver value faster. However, it's highly unlikely that composite applications will replace legacy, but we will see the rise of such application types in portfolios. Organizations do not operate in a Greenfield development model and must accommodate the need to leverage legacy systems.

51. Is a Certain Type of Business Problem Best Suited for SOA Adoption?

All applications can be designed based on the concept of service orientation, and they can be composed as a set of services or composite services. It is not feasible to transition all applications to a new architecture such as SOA, nor is it advisable. In addition, SOA is not a panacea, and some problems are better suited for SOA than others. That is, certain business characteristics, if present, make the case for SOA more likely, as illustrated in Figure 6.2. This model can be used to make a decision about adopting SOA when constructing a new application, transforming an application, or procuring a new application. In Figure 6.2, those business attributes trending to the right are more likely SOA candidate projects. Just answering a series of questions using this model can yield a position about whether the project is suitable for SOA:

- **How much change is anticipated or expected for the business process?** Business processes that expect a lot of change (for example, new process changes must be deployed into production every three months) require more agility than processes that change less frequently. Business processes that must accommodate unknown changes in the future require more flexibility. For example, regional differences can make claim adjudication processing look different based on whether the claim is filed in California versus Illinois. In California, the claim experience accommodates a regulatory requirement that prescriptions be treated the same as doctor visits when processing deductibles. In Colorado, prescriptions can have higher deductibles than doctor visits. In this example, 50 different regions combined with frequent changes in regulations requires claims processing be adjusted every few months. The regional and regulatory variances can be handled by using services to address externalizing rules from the application or using services for process configuration changes. Or, take the case where an organization expands its business model from a focus purely on high net worth clients and small businesses to any retail customers with different risk and financial profiles. Adopting SOA allows the application to accommodate changes to the business process to service this new capability rather than the company deciding they need two applications—one for high net worth customers, and another for all retail customers.

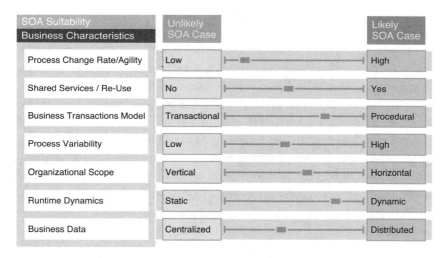

Figure 6.2   Judging SOA suitability by looking at business characteristics

- **Does specific business functionality have to support multiple applications or multiple business processes?** Update address or retrieve customer information are typical examples of business functionality that must be frequently invoked, by many applications. Companies prefer to have only one instance of the code base rather than have the code redundantly housed in multiple applications, making changing it more expensive and time consuming.

- **Is the transactional model more procedural (i.e., human centric) or system centric (i.e., transactional)?** Does the main functionality depend on throughput? For example, an authorization switch that authorizes and denies credit or debit card transactions by operating as an intermediary between the merchant's systems and the institution that provides the credit/debit card could be described as system centric because transactions occur system to system. Throughput requirements are high; millions of transactions must be processed per hour. Contrast this to a customer service application where a person is needed to both engage with the customer and navigate multiple processes or systems. The procedural-centric attribute is a greater candidate for SOA because change is more likely to accommodate ever-changing channels (e.g., mobile devices or new market segmentations) and changing customer demands. Transactional-centric systems might benefit from aspects of SOA adoption, but performance demands or other performance characteristics might limit the range of SOA attributes that should be applied.

- **Is there a need to support different process execution models, perhaps due to geographic differences?** For example, regulations and country-specific laws make it necessary to deal with process variances. It is preferred that these variances not be hard-coded so that the base application can be reused. The more variances, the more likely SOA will be a good fit for applications that automate such processes.

- **Does the business functionality have to be accessed and used across organizational boundaries?** In many cases, especially customer service applications, organizations want customers to have the same experience whether they are in the United States or Europe, and whether they are engaged with the loans division or credit card. When processes are horizontal in nature, such as a self-service portal for handling exceptions, the application architecture must accommodate different user interfaces, different channels, and different workflows. Providing the ability to assemble services into different workflows or plug into different user interface contexts allows the process and user interface to work dependently or independently as needed by the business. The consumer creates the workflow based on their user experience rather than a hard-wired application with a predetermined process or workflow.

- **Do process execution alternatives vary depending on business context?** That is, do runtime policies (e.g., business rules) determine the process flow? Is the capability to dynamically influence the processing of already existing structured business processes for specific events required? Is there a need for business process policies, business rules, business event processing? An example of using business events and rules might be to address debit and credit card theft. For example, whenever a cumulative debit over $200 USD in a 7-day window for any network address originates in certain countries, deny the debit. A context-aware debit service that is sensitized to location will render different results. Whenever rules or policies need to be inspected at run time, it suggests a good case for the use of services.

- **Is there a need to provide a holistic or single, timely, and accurate view of information (e.g., single customer view) where the data sources are currently found in multiple sources?** Often due to silos and challenges in integration, multiple data sources evolve reflecting customer data. In many organizations, this problem can be traced to its source where customer data is captured; data capture occurs in several places using different applications and databases. The result is often multiple data sources with customer information. Which one has the correct address or the correct spelling of the name? SOA, using information services, can provide a single "truth." For example, many companies have different silos that capture information about the same customer such as name and address. Consuming applications that need to obtain a customer address should use the getAddress information service that deals with underlying differences in data sources and the multiple applications.

Answering this series of questions enables stakeholders to make an informed decision about the suitability of SOA as an architectural approach for various types of applications.

52. Is a Certain Type of IT Problem Best Suited for SOA Adoption?

In addition to the business characteristics, organizations should examine IT characteristics, as illustrated in Figure 6.3. Answering the following questions using the model illustrated in Figure 6.3 yields a suitability score for determining whether to adopt SOA for a project:

- **Are there a high number of interfaces?** When organizations are looking at integrating three or more systems and this number is growing, it represents an opportunity for considering SOA for integration. The corresponding question is whether the underlying technology to perform the integration must be changed each time.

- **Is the complexity of the external interface high?** For example, there is a high demand for data transformation between systems each time the application requires integration with new systems.

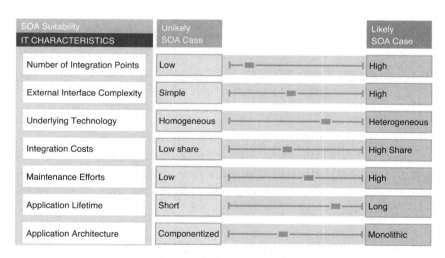

Figure 6.3 SOA suitability: looking at IT characteristics

- **Is the underlying technology model homogeneous (e.g., hardware and software stack is largely sourced from a single vendor) or heterogeneous (e.g., deployed hardware and software stack comprises multiple vendors)?** Heterogeneous environments often mean greater complexity of the integration, and this cost is repeatedly incurred per integration. Adopting SOA simplifies the integration.

- **Are integration costs rising?** For many organizations, substantial amounts of the IT spent in running the business are incurred in integration costs. SOA adoption can lower these costs.

- **Are the maintenance costs high?** That is, the maintenance costs do not include enhancements but defect repairs or rework. Costs can also be high if multiple applications are being maintained and supported even though they perform similar tasks.

- **What is the expected life of the application?** Applications that have an expected short life (e.g., less than two years) may not warrant an investment in architecture. Similarly to building a house, if it will be torn down in a year or abandoned in two years, investing in a blueprint for longevity and change is not warranted.

- **Is the current application componentized or monolithic?** Application architectures that can easily change do not warrant a change in architectural approaches. Such applications might use aspects of SOA in their construction, such as exposing services outside the enterprise firewalls to partners or suppliers.

The SOA suitability models for business and IT should be used as guidelines, not a litmus test. By assessing a future project using both business and IT attributes, organizations can make informed and guided decisions about when to pursue SOA as a strategy and architectural approach.

53. What Changes with Application Development When SOA Is Introduced?

The use of a consistent method to develop appropriately sized, partitioned, and shared services that have undergone the necessary variation analysis is a significant change with the introduction of SOA. Chapter 5, "Methods," addresses several system development issues.

Other changes relate to how the development process gets integrated with tooling to address issues such as what services go into the service registry. Addressing how services are managed by policies and the use of rules engines, policy managers, and BPM technology for process orchestration are changes to application development. In addition, the use of a shared integration infrastructure, ESB, is another change. Applications use the ESB for services in much the same way applications use databases for data. In both cases, there is a need to work in a shared environment, share models (e.g., message versus data schemas), a common shared infrastructure (e.g., ESB versus database), and to collaborate to understand how to leverage what already exists (e.g., service modelers/service designers versus data modelers / DBAs).

Thinking about services and what services are needed versus what are the functional requirements is a different approach brought about by SOA thinking in application development. Most application development projects capture a large set of functional requirements, often because of how application projects are identified, selected, and funded. For example, the investment is approved at a coarse level for a new claims system versus defining a need for a consistent membership service. It is only natural to define requirements at a functional level, often for a coarse grain, monolithic, silo application. Embracing SOA at the business and application level requires a shift from functional, silo thinking to domain thinking where the services are identified and directly related to business models (e.g., process or information). Approaching the capture of requirements through services requires behavior and cultural changes in how business and IT relate to each and how functional requirements are articulated.

Functional requirements can be captured in different artifacts, such as use cases, functional specifications, or requirements documents. The problem is not with any of these specific artifacts per se but with how functional requirements are captured and translated into design specifications for coding. Figure 6.4 shows a typical relationship between business processes and applications, where applications typically satisfy one or more activities in a business process. In most organizations, a use case is developed to capture the business process, its flow, and control. In Figure 6.4, the use case would describe the flow between processes A through I. Use cases or functional requirements documents also specify the user interface navigation, screen flow, or as some describe, what happens on the glass. Use cases describe process variations, business rules, and data needs. Capturing this range of functional requirements (process flow, screen flow, control and flow logic, process variations, business rules, and data) as a single set of functional requirements or use cases entrenches application silos and increases tight coupling downstream in the software design.

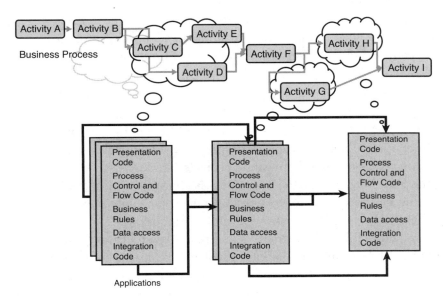

Figure 6.4   Business processes and applications

Using a simple example, let's illustrate why this approach to specifying business requirements creates tighter coupling of software components during design and entrenches application silos. Suppose the business process in Figure 6.4 represented an exception process for handling claims. The claims exception process has several activities, one of which is to collect information on the claim by a claim agent from customers; another activity is to create a claim folder for holding this and other information about the claim. The claim folder can be used throughout the claims process life cycle to house claim information allowing for a long-living process that might span days or weeks. Whenever claim information is collected, a claim folder is needed to store the claim information so that the persistent data is available throughout the process. The claim information is available for multiple claim agents who might be helping a single customer who is trying to get money to rebuild their house after a fire. Business stakeholders may specify as a requirement that whenever a request is made to get claim information, the system should build a claim folder. The application designer takes this statement, "create claim folder whenever a request to get claim information," as a requirement and fulfills it by designing two components—get claim information and create claim folder—that are coupled. Neither the business stakeholder or application designer can see a situation where a request for getting claim information would be done outside the context of creating a claim folder for later resolution. However, the business does change, and a need for a cross selling insurance application arises, which requires access to claim information, but not for the purpose of creating a claim. Reusing the get claim information function will be difficult if it is encased in an application silo. In order to reuse the get claim information function, a change must be made to stop creating claim folders whenever a request is made to get claim information; otherwise, the system might drown in a sea of empty claim folders. This example illustrates downstream coupling that occurs in the code base as a result of how requirements are articulated.

If a service was the design point for establishing functional boundaries, this coupling could be avoided. Using SOA, two services would be created: getClaimInfo and createClaimFolder. Both services would be loosely coupled (no dependency on the other) and sharable. With SOA and services, the new cross-selling application would consume the getClaimInfo service without a need for any application integration or modifications to the existing claims processing application. This requires that services be identified early in the life cycle, and functional requirements would be organized accordingly—that is, each service would have its on set of functional requirements.

Using services introduces new artifacts in the application development cycle, illustrated in Figure 6.5. Although this is not a complete list of new artifacts, it does highlight the need for a service model, candidate services, for which there will be use cases. Services provide functional structure, separation of concerns along functional boundaries, and services structure the component model which in turn provides the boundaries for structuring object classes. Organizations that pursue business architectures should also understand their portfolio of business services that can be used to improve business processes and create new solutions. Information models, when present, can provide the basis for database design and canonical message models for deriving message schemas for service interactions.

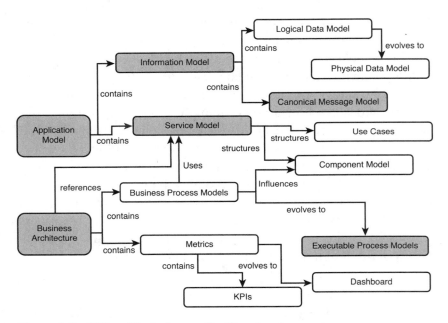

Figure 6.5   SOA artifacts for application development

The focus in SOA for application development shifts to using services to define scope and boundaries of a development effort and for requirements. The focus is on the set of business-aligned services (i.e., business services) that collectively enable the fulfillment of business goals; the services can be recombined in unanticipated business contexts. Instead of being simply a user interacting with a system, it can be seen as an ecosystem of providers and consumers with interchangeable roles that leverage the services. Scoping the delivery of the application to align with the requirements of the business, using services, provides a flexibility characteristic to application development as the application architecture gets organized in business terms. This change will be one of the most difficult for organizations to make—a shift from functional silo thinking to service-oriented thinking.

Application development activities that are focused on architecture, requirements, development, and testing undergo change with SOA adoption. Chapter 5, "Methods," provides details about the specific changes in these areas using the context of methods to describe the changes. Organizations seeking the sustained business benefits of SOA described in Chapter 1, "SOA Basics," will see cultural change around reuse, as assembly of services gets blended with the custom build of new services. Relationships between business stakeholders who provide business requirements and IT providers who satisfy these requirements will use services as a major construct. Designers and developers must understand and adopt open standards (such as web services and REST), new development tools (such as registry), and new runtime tools addressing security, governance, and management of services.

One additional change concerns metrics. Metrics should be captured and managed as part of the application development cycle. Project managers should be asked to measure the number of services reused, savings from reuse, and the number of new reusable services created. Metrics are a gauge, which is continuously adjusted, rather than a lever, which has a right or wrong association.

54. What Is the Relationship of Business Process Management to an Application?

Business Process Management (BPM) is a management discipline focused on the following:

- Aligning business process performance and the results with strategic objectives and business goals
- Understanding and documenting business processes so that they may be consistently executed
- Measuring, monitoring, and controlling process performance, including key inputs and outputs

- Actively designing and improving business processes to meet or exceed the expectations of customers while achieving business goals (e.g., cost and revenue)

BPM solutions vary from a focus on human-centric business processes, to document and content-focus processes, to structure and system-oriented processes.

A business process can be represented as collaboration between components, as illustrated in Figure 6.5. A customer who wants a loan walks into a bank or calls a loan broker, and a business process begins. The customer completes a loan application as a first step of the process. Before the customer's loan application is approved, a series of activities must be completed. Unknown to the customer, one or more applications may be necessary to complete the business process—that is, the business funding the loan uses a variety of tools (e.g., applications) as part of the loan process. Applications are used to automate business processes or activities of a process such as the loan underwriting application. Each activity of the business process, such as check credit history or setup loan account, could also be a service. The business process, submit loan application, may also be expressed as a service. BPM solutions can be used instead of custom-coded applications to model and automate the submit loan application. BPM solutions can be as light as helping with expressing the business model or as robust as automating and monitoring the submit loan process. When fully automated, for example, the customer might receive an alert or text message, notifying them that their loan was approved. Or if the loan exceeds a service level established by the business of always processing loans within ten days, an alert could be sent to a manager notifying her on the eighth day that the loan is unlikely to be completed in a ten-day window.

SOA helps make the underlying technology that supports BPM and the business process less rigid and more agile by allowing the business process, or any activity of the business process, to be expressed as services. Applications that use BPM technologies often represent a set of orchestrated, loosely coupled services that are called in a certain sequence optimally designed to support business process. Business processes that leverage services or BPM technology can be easily monitored. In other words, key performance indicators (KPIs) can be defined for how long a process takes to complete a given task or around whether a process successfully completes a transaction and how often. The tracking and measurement of KPIs is done through business activity monitoring, where business analytics are critical to confirm that business performance is on track.

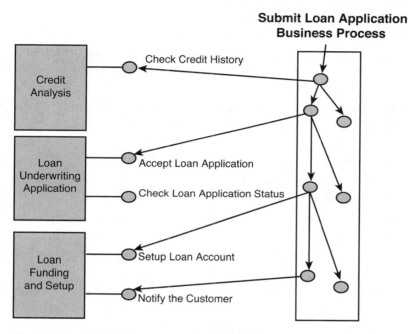

Figure 6.6   Business Process and Applications

Often, with regard to the discipline of BPM (life cycle and methods related to modeling, process execution, and monitoring), the tools that enable the discipline and business process solutions are used interchangeably, confusing the matter as to the relationship to SOA. BPM can be both a business discipline and a software engineering discipline. In the former, the business takes an active role in business process management, and IT takes an active role in providing enabling technologies to support BPM as a business discipline. When BPM is a software engineering discipline, it involves the use of standards and the use of BPM-enabling technologies. As a software engineering discipline, the submit loan application business process is designed to use BPM technologies for its automation or a hybrid of custom code, legacy systems, and BPM technologies. The software engineering aspects make choices on what aspects of the code base should be provisioned using BPM technology, such as a workflow or custom code as services, or integrate with existing legacy systems.

Several challenges are presented when applications and business processes are co-mingled or tightly coupled. Figure 6.4 illustrates the business process, applications, and the need to integrate applications with one another to fulfill a business process. Often, the ability to monitor the business process end-to-end is lacking, with monitoring fulfilled by multiple applications where each has its own view. The business process is often buried or locked in the application, fragmenting the business process and making it less likely to have a holistic view of the process. Little commonality exists across applications, as they each have their own presentation, data, and business rules. Adopting BPM can make it easier to create, monitor, and react to event information or use analytics to improve the performance of the business process.

For years, BPM was viewed solely as the creation and customization of applications. Over time, business process logic became more deeply embedded in these customized applications, locked away in millions of lines of often undocumented code and proprietary data structures that were slow, risky, and expensive to change. To make matters worse, as change became more difficult, the frequently chosen path was to duplicate business functionality, which of course increased the difficulty and expense of changing the code. The result is higher IT costs and lower productivity, growing IT project backlogs, and the inability to respond to new or changing market opportunities. Adding to this problem is the business cost of manual workarounds and the impact of bad or stale data on decision-making, and the picture gets bleaker. Advances in disciplines, architectures, and technologies in both SOA and BPM are allowing IT budgets to be reclaimed and organizations to be repositioned. These advances unlock existing application functionality to greatly accelerate process improvement and innovation. Hence, BPM and SOA are often "joined at the hip" when it comes to increasing business value.

55. How Does SOA Make Applications or a Portfolio of Applications More Flexible?

SOA provides several value drivers for making both an application and an application portfolio more flexible. These values, each of which improves flexibility, include the following:

- **Flexibility as measured by time and cost avoidance**
  Reduce future development time
  Reduce future development cost
  Reduce risk of obsolescence
  Reduce future business operating cost

- **Flexibility as measured by time and cost improvement**
  Reduce development time
  Reduce development cost
  Reduce IT maintenance cost
  Reduce error rate

- **Business process management flexibility by improving the ease of business integration**
  Reduce development time
  Reduce development cost

Chapter 2, "Business," provides a more detailed explanation about how each of these business benefits accrues with SOA adoption. Each of the benefits reflects a future cost, whether that is the cost avoidance to deal with change or the present cost savings in efficiency or reuse. In Figure 6.7, the SOA solution comes with an option to change, although both the non-SOA solution and the SOA solution provide equivalent business functionality. In the non-SOA solution, the ability to change or upgrade is most often cost-prohibitive or untimely. If the business or environment does not change, the non-SOA solution is quite satisfactory. SOA solutions are built to change, and most likely will require more investment than a non-SOA solution, but for solutions that need to be built for change, the SOA solution will pay longer term benefits to the business in addition to meeting tactical concerns.

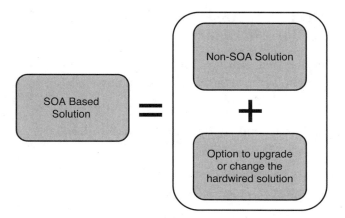

Figure 6.7   SOA Built-in option to change

The option to change is engineered in SOA solutions; Figure 6.8 illustrates a spectrum of flexibility provided by an SOA. Each improvement of software engineering has improved application flexibility that is reflected in widely used application programming interfaces. The use of data formats and databases increased flexibility further as applications began to share common data schemas that were no longer entirely hardwired in the application, but were live independently and shared by multiple applications as the industry moved to databases. EAI introduced more flexibility and the advent of services, and ESBs pushed the flexibility more to the right. Services increase application flexibility with a semantic interface where with services a business language semantic is used (e.g., retrieve balance) versus the desired functionality being encoded in the message that is sent requesting the balance. Self-describing data allows people and machines to read and interpret data streams. The option to change for SOA is reflected in the use of services, service semantic interface, canonical message formats, service interface, self-describing data, and the use of ESBs for integration and sharing of services.

SOA solutions make applications and application portfolios more flexible by engineering the applications to change, which means engineering loose coupling, componentized versus monolithic applications, independent test cycles, reuse at the organization level versus individual programmer, and engineered as an attribute of the solution (not an inspection process). SOA promotes service interfaces that separate application logic from business process, allowing each to evolve independently. Monolithic applications can't be easily reused because business functionality is locked in the application. In many cases, the business process is constrained by the application code base where IT tells the business what can and cannot be done. In addition, ad hoc integration creates connections that are difficult to change and maintain. SOA decomposes monolithic applications into services along functional boundaries that promote loose coupling, and improved cohesion, all of which makes applications easier to change and more flexible.

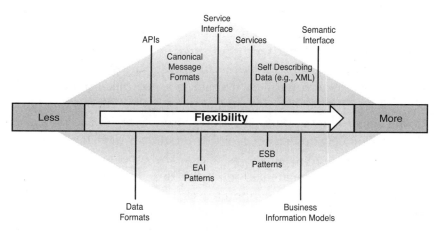

Figure 6.8   SOA influence on flexibility

56. Should an Application Portfolio Be Managed Differently Because of SOA Adoption?

With SOA, application portfolios are augmented with a service portfolio. Organizations can now use a service portfolio as the central point of developing business functionality and business capabilities. Instead of making investment requests for new applications, organizations would make investment cases for new or modified business processes or new business services. This requires a culture change for most organizations because today, companies approach their investment strategies and prioritization along functional boundaries that translate to requests for new or modified applications. Application portfolios and a service portfolio will co-exist. The management of application portfolios should be modified to reflect the existence of a service portfolio where investment and prioritization includes thinking about directing the reuse of services and the provisioning of new services, not just applications. In Figure 6.6, the modified process for funding and investing in new applications would shift to recognizing that services exist for checking credit history, accepting new loan applications, or opening a loan account. Management of the application portfolio should change to recognize a shared service portfolio. Executives and managers must encourage or mandate the reuse of existing services in the service portfolio, and fund new services or modifications to existing services.

The focus of prioritization and project selection shifts from silo applications to a categorized list of services. With SOA, the time to uncover and categorize the necessary list of capabilities required to support a particular business domain is a new management discipline. It requires a change to current practices for funding and identifying what to buy or build. A request for new services accompanies requests for new applications, and it requires a repeatable process that delivers from a catalog of services. The process must take into account "does this functionality exist already in the form of a service," and if not, initiate the service lifecycle of provisioning or reusing existing services. The service inventories generated from each portfolio need to be leveraged as part of the organizational reuse strategy. This reuse strategy is not much different from what occurs today when organizations decide to enhance an existing application, which is another way of saying let's reuse the existing application.

57. Can Existing Systems or Legacy Applications Be Leveraged When Adopting SOA?

Applications, once deployed into production, are considered legacy. Legacy applications like CRM and ERP can be package implementations or custom-built applications. Legacy as a term carries a perception that it is difficult to change and improve; that is, legacy can translate to a burden ("bad legacy") or mean heritage ("good legacy"). Legacy applications are treated differently depending on the burden or heritage aspects. It is unlikely that we will see legacy applications, which are burdens, evolve into composite applications that are assembled. Instead, new and emerging technologies (e.g., mobile and cloud computing) and new business realities (e.g., crowd sourcing or globalization) will mandate transformations of "burden" legacy systems to adopt SOA and employ services or composite services where facades and wrappers will be used to extend "bad legacy" by encapsulating business function into services. Companies creating new applications will adopt SOA to avoid heritage applications from becoming "bad legacy."

One of the many advantages of SOA is the potential to leverage legacy systems. SOA adoption does not mean that the application portfolio will consist entirely of services to the exclusion of all else. This is a common misconception. Legacy systems need to be leveraged and prior investments need to be capitalized upon. SOA accomplishes this goal by incrementally integrating existing systems with services at key functional points where business capabilities tend to change. If a section of the business process is pretty constant and not prone to change, service enablement of that portion may be deferred to another time. Figure 6.6 shows multiple process steps, each of which represents a functional point. In this example, perhaps checking credit history and setup of a loan account has been constant for a number of years, but the accepting loan application is constantly being modified because of changing technology. It started with paper, moved to online form entry, and now loan applications can be submitted via mobile devices. Making accept loan application a service might be a step in making the legacy application more flexible and a step toward SOA adoption. It's fairly typical for most transformations of legacy to start with the aspects of the application that are customer facing or the business to consumer model.

Wrapping online transactions with services often provides the benefit of making legacy systems' business functionality more widely accessible, but it does not repair existing issues of underlying fragmentation of existing code bases, poorly aligned data structures, disparate date sources, or redundancy in the application portfolio. However, a phased and incremental approach to the transformation or modernization of existing legacy systems can provide a reusable portfolio of services where SOA benefits come to fruition. The phasing and prioritization should be determined by budgetary constraints, business imperatives, and the degrees of agility, reuse, and business performance desired. Those portions of the legacy code base that perform a specific function and are being changed more frequently than other portions of code within the application should be refactored, externalized, and service-enabled in a systematic fashion using SOA.

The adoption of SOA for legacy can start with one application becoming partially service-enabled by using patterns. One such pattern is a virtual provider pattern in which the assumption is that the boundaries of your application are only going to be service-enabled. So when integrating with other applications, although the other application is not SOA-enabled, you still make a service invocation using a virtual service provider pattern.

This virtual service provider acts as a proxy from inside your application. It makes it look as if you are making a service call to the other application, but in fact you are using a virtual service provider snippet of code. In this way, even though you do not have funding to service-enable all the applications that your application will call or require, you can gradually ramp up and bootstrap the service-enablement effort in the organization by preparing an application to call other applications through a virtual provider.

58. How Are Services Built That Will Deploy in a Cloud?

The "cloud" refers to a virtual infrastructure in which dynamically scalable, virtualized resources are provided as a service over the Internet. With cloud computing, organizations choose between renting an application, process, service, or infrastructure or completely outsourcing one or more of these aspects to a cloud provider.

Loose coupling is a key litmus test for services being deployed in a cloud. That is, the optimal scenario for moving services to a cloud is when one can bundle five fundamental elements of SOA and deploy them as an independent unit. These five elements are a set of services, components, processes, data, and rules that are closely aligned with one another and are collectively more loosely coupled and less dependent on other groups of services, components, processes, data, and rules.

One of the key principles and value propositions of SOA is its geographic independence. This geographic autonomy implies that the services clustered together are not in themselves bound to a data center or geographic location. Instead, they can indeed be deployed within a cloud that may span multiple smaller cloud structures, starting from inside a private cloud and moving into a public cloud and hybrid cloud architecture to suit security, performance, and scalability requirements and service-level requirements or agreements. Cloud computing provides new architectural deployment options for services.

The adoption of services requires increased thinking about security, and the use of cloud services further increases the risk of having non-secured services. The Cloud Security Alliance (CSA) has created a controls matrix to address the security risks by a cloud provider. Services in the cloud must be secured.

59. Does It Make Sense to Adopt SOA for One Application Versus the Enterprise?

A gradual and incremental approach to service adoption is a prudent way to introduce and adopt SOA. A critical mass of skills developed through a set of change agents within an organization is often required to scale to an enterprise scale. SOA can and should begin with projects that demonstrate cost benefits, increasing flexibility, faster time to market, and ultimately better business performance overall. This often translates into incremental adoption of SOA, where each project adds to a portfolio of services accessible across organizational boundaries and at the enterprise level. The SOA infrastructure expands by project and by each application usage, and an enterprise focus is required to ensure reusability of the infrastructures such that silos don't develop; after all, silos fragment the advantages of a shared infrastructure and thus diminish the cost benefits of a shared infrastructure. In other words, if everyone builds their own infrastructure, their own ESB, then it becomes more difficult to share services, and the cost of the total cost of ownership of the infrastructure is not optimized over time. The service registry and ESB require an enterprise focus so that the value related to reuse and lower cost could be sustained. So, it can make sense to adopt SOA at a project or application level, but there has to be an enterprise focus at the same time.

60. What Are Common Pitfalls for Application Teams Adopting SOA?

The most common pitfalls that application managers and application teams involved in SOA adoption see are related to not recognizing or not planning for the following:

- SOA is a paradigm shift.
- SOA is a journey.
- SOA benefits accrue only with improved collaboration between business and IT.

SOA is a paradigm shift. The implication is that the advantages of SOA, in areas of agility, reuse, accelerated development, lower cost, and variability, will not be realized if the same application development practices are adopted. If application teams build the same way as before, it's likely and probable that the end results will have the same quality. Adoption of the SOA-based methods, SOA reference architecture, SOA governance, and rescaling or augmenting the skills of different roles within the organization are gradual changes that should be understood and accommodated. Applications should no longer be built as silos. Application architectures tend to originate in a specific line of business within the context of a specific project, and this will gradually change. Focusing exclusively on the sole concerns of just one line of business often leads to the phenomenon of developing silo application architectures and applications themselves.

Prepare for the SOA journey; it's going to take more than a day. The adoption of new disciplines, practices, and technologies helps bridge IT and business; and it requires planning and continuous monitoring to achieve the maximum results. Organizations with a clear SOA strategy or SOA vision that articulates the goals, current issues, business scenarios, architecture vision for the future, metrics, and roadmap will see much greater success than organizations that treat each of these activities ad hoc. Adopting a clear set of metrics upfront requires business goals and a vision, to demonstrate that you have actually achieved the goals and objectives of your journey. A journey needs a destination (in this case, an objective), and if you cannot measure that objective, it's not likely organizations will know whether the objective has been achieved. In turn, this makes sustaining the journey difficult and challenging as funding and resources dwindle if the business cannot see or measure the business value return. Change agents, organization and cultural change, cannot be underestimated, because this is both an ongoing and required activity throughout the journey.

Collaboration between business and IT must often adjust to the new paradigm. Most companies that have spent years adopting SOA are still on a journey to improve the dialog between business and IT development. Very few organizations have metrics to legitimize the SOA claims and manage business expectations. Business and IT must have a collaborative and solid working relationship of shared responsibility for SOA to meet its promises. Technology-only efforts are ultimately doomed to failure if success is measured as making the promises of SOA come to fruition. This is especially true if an organization's funding comes from the business side. Therefore, for the business to gain the maximum benefit, or in fact any short-term benefit, the business should invest in IT's capability to meet changing requirements and implement those changes in a time-sensitive fashion that is not cost prohibitive and does not produce large ripple effects not only on the technology side but with the business consequences.

Applications: Key Concepts

Applications remain as a concept with SOA, with the major change to applications being the use of services as the major restructuring element for them. Services can be atomic or composite. SOA methods will play a major role in the successful identification and granularity of services. Breaking application business functionality into smaller pieces or building blocks that can be reassembled, rearranged, and reused easily provides benefits for accelerating application development. SOA has the opportunity to reduce the cost of maintaining an application and accelerating application development through reuse and to improve efficiencies. However, SOA requires a paradigm shift, and applications teams must adopt a different approach for developing applications, using services, if the promises of SOA are to be realized. Application teams must address SOA governance where organizational change, cultural change, method change, and architectural changes occur.

SOA and BPM represent disciplined improvement methodologies, which may be linked together to drive higher levels of effectiveness, efficiency, and business outcomes. As service reuse rises, IT costs go down, and future process changes can occur more quickly. The objective of SOA for applications is to drive custom coding down and raise the amount of reuse. IT backlogs, budget constraints, and the tendency to favor tactical concerns over strategic concerns will continue to be an issue for organizations and application teams pursuing SOA. Measuring and communicating value and success is a necessity for application managers. The inability to mandate a strategy, like SOA, will require tough choices along the way for SOA adoption to take hold.

7

Architecture

Software entities are more complex for their size than perhaps any other human construct. It is inherent because it reflects the complexity of human instituuwebtions, not the simplicity of nature, as the laws of physics do. Many of the classic problems of developing software products derive from this essential complexity and its nonlinear increases with size.

—Frederick P. Brooks

Architecture is about providing balance in the face of conflicting concerns. Software entities, architectures, have gotten more complex as we have progressed from monolithic to client/server to network-centric architectures and now to service-oriented architectures. Architectural evolution continues to move toward agility and hence the attention and interest in SOA. At the heart of every new shift in architecture sits a practically or theoretically compelling concept that brings the paradigm forward. Client/server introduced the distributed application architecture that portioned workloads between service providers and service consumers referred to as clients. Network-centric architectures introduced the Internet as a paradigm shift. Now with SOA, services are the architectural game changer, moving the architecture to greater agility.

We started coding in objects after procedural programming and structured design had evolved. Object-oriented programming gave way to the need to design using objects, and then a plethora of object-oriented analysis and design methods and techniques ensued: Rumbaugh, Jacobson, Coad, Wirfs-Brock, and others. Eventually, patterns evolved that took smaller units of programming and built micro architectures that were dubbed design patterns. One of the programming notions that developed into a best practice in object orientation was "program to interfaces, not to implementations." This separation of concerns allowed greater underlying flexibility in development: both at design time (classification and class associations) and runtime (polymorphism).

With the evolution of objects came the need to group them into larger-grained entities and to build larger-grained components. Component-based development, and later component-based design, created larger structures that were more closely mapped to business intent and needs. When Web services—with the promise of looser coupling and greater standardization than the Common Object Request Broker Architecture (CORBA) or Distributed Computing Environment (DCE)—came to the forefront and promised to make distributed computing more accessible, programmers started to build remote procedure calls with XML-based objects. As the momentum grew, Web services architecture gave way to SOA.

As we seek to handle complexity in building software systems, we encounter various architectural styles better suited to solving a certain class of problems. For example, pipes and filters, black-board architectures, layered architectures, and so on all have been used to solve specific problems in specific domains. However, other architectural styles provide a greater degree of general utility. In other words, the use of that architectural style is not necessarily limited to solving specific problems within specific domains. Instead, foundational elements of the solutions provided by that architectural style find their way into the foundations of software architecture, rather than being confined to alleviating problems in a specific domain. When developing software systems, service-oriented thinking pushes the boundaries of traditional software architecture and provides new insights into handling complexity, thus deriving commonality and increasing agility. This chapter examines many of the key architectural concerns of SOA and answers several key questions pertaining to IT architecture:

61. How does architecture change as a result of SOA adoption?

62. How does SOA differ from earlier approaches, such as DCE or CORBA?

63. How do Web services and SOA differ?

64. Is SOA too complex and enterprise level only?

65. How do interfaces and contracts differ?

66. Should applications choose WSDL or REST?

67. What is the relationship between enterprise architecture and SOA?

68. How do EAI, SOA, and SOI differ from one another?

69. What is the role of standards in SOA implementations?

70. How should standards be applied to enable successful SOA implementations?

71. What are the common pitfalls when adapting or changing the IT architecture for SOA?

Architecture: Q&A

61. How Does Architecture Change as a Result of SOA Adoption?

The notion of "program to interfaces" has gradually elevated to an architectural construct: the services layer in the application or solution architecture. A new tier or layer has emerged, and it's dedicated to services, which include contracts, interfaces, and service descriptions. With this emergence came another realization: The ways in which practitioners discover and identify objects and classes started to break down when identifying services in SOA. Thus, services gained the status of a first-class construct in software engineering and became a primary concern for application architecture as a result of SOA. So, there are three major changes to architecture:

- Use of contracts in addition to interfaces in the architecture and program design
- Adoption of shared services for improved integration and structuring applications
- Use of a services layer to increase flexibility in systems and applications

Contracts and interfaces are different, and SOA leverages both. However, design by contract provides increased flexibility because it promotes repeatable results and loose coupling between the requester and provider. The details of this specific difference are covered in a later question in this chapter.

The adoption of shared services for improved integration and structuring using services engineers flexibility into application architectures. Application architecture can use services or be structured using services; the latter provides the greatest infusion of flexibility because it has an architecture that is built for change. When a business process and its supporting application are represented as a set of services, it affords the opportunity to access those services independently of the channel (such as the mobile device, Internet, kiosk, system, or others) and workflow, so that business capability is not locked within the application. Access to capabilities or business functions is not restricted to a predefined process workflow or user experience (that is, screen flow). Services provide a means to readily access the functionality when needed and wherever required.

Figure 7.1 describes several layers and their relationships as the primary distinctive qualities of SOA. That is, by reviewing these layers, the question about what is architecturally different as a result of SOA adoption is answered. Figure 7.1 illustrates these layers:

- **Layer 1: Operational Systems.** This layer includes all custom or packaged applications and systems in the application portfolio running in an IT operating environment and supporting business activities.

- **Layer 2: Service Component Layer.** This layer contains software components, each of which provides the implementation for or "realizes" a service or operation on a service (hence, the name service component).

- **Layer 3: Services Layer.** This layer consists of all services within the SOA: service descriptions, policies, versions of a service, SOA management descriptions, and attachments that categorize or show service dependencies.

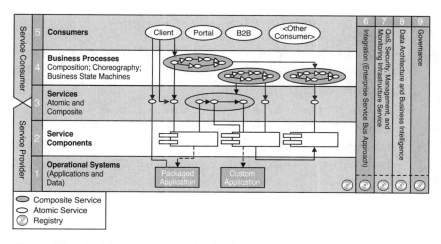

Figure 7.1 Architecture layers for SOA

- **Layer 4: Business Process Layer.** Compositions and choreographies of services exposed in Layer 3 are defined in this layer. The evolution of service composition into flows or choreographies of services bundled into a flow act together to establish an application. These applications support specific use cases and business processes. Here, visual flow composition tools can be used for design of application flow.

- **Layer 5: Consumer Layer.** This layer provides the capabilities required to deliver IT functions and data to end users that meet specific usage preferences. SOA decouples the user interface from the components.

- **Layer 6: Integration Layer.** This layer is a key enabler for SOA, providing the capability to mediate, route, and transport service requests from the service requester to the correct service provider.

- **Layer 7: Quality of Service Layer.** Inherent in SOA are characteristics that exacerbate existing QoS concerns in computer systems: Increased virtualization/loose coupling, widespread use of XML, the composition of federated services, heterogeneous computing infrastructures, decentralized *service level agreements* (SLAs), the need to aggregate IT QoS metrics to produce business metrics, and so on are the nature of SOA. These characteristics create complications for QoS that clearly require attention in any SOA solution.

- **Layer 8: Data Architecture and Business Intelligence Layer.** The Data Architecture and Business Intelligence Layer ensures the inclusion of key considerations pertaining to data architecture and information architectures that can also be used as the basis for the creation of business intelligence through data marts and data warehouses. This includes meta-data content that is stored in this layer.

- **Layer 9: SOA Governance Layer.** This layer covers all aspects of business operational life cycle management in SOA. It provides guidance and policies for managing all the aspects of services, SLA, capacity and performance, security, and monitoring in SOA solutions. This layer emphasizes operational life cycle management.

The Operational Systems Layer, Layer 1, consists of the different running (operational) software systems, including custom monolithic applications, legacy applications, transaction processing applications, database management systems, *enterprise resource planning* (ERP) systems, *customer relationship management* (CRM) packages and solutions, and the runtime environment required for these systems. The operating system environments and the associated hardware platforms are all part of this layer, but are not explicitly called out diagrammatically. This layer is a foundational layer and includes all the runtime environments required for services to be operational in an SOA. The characteristics and responsibilities of the Operational Systems Layer influence the success of a deployed SOA. The Operational Systems Layer consists of existing hardware and software systems, thereby leveraging existing IT investments to implement SOA solutions. This directly influences the overall cost of implementing SOA solutions within enterprises and also frees parts of the overall budget for newer initiatives and development of business-critical services.

The Service Component Layer, Layer 2, manifests the IT conformance with each service contract defined in the Services Layer; it guarantees the alignment of IT implementation with service description. Each service component provides an enforcement point for "faithful" service realization (ensure QoS and SLAs) and enables business flexibility by supporting the functional implementation of IT flexible services, their composition, and layering. IT flexibility is strengthened through the decoupling in the system. Decoupling is achieved by hiding volatile implementation details from consumers.

The Services Layer, Layer 3, contains exposed services that can be "discovered" and invoked, or possibly choreographed, to create a composite service. Services are "functions" that are accessible across a network via well-defined interfaces of the Services Layer. The Services Layer also provides for the mechanism to take enterprise-scale components, business unit-specific components, and in some cases project-specific components and externalize a subset of their interfaces in the form of service descriptions. Thus, the components provide services through their interfaces. The interfaces get exported out as service descriptions in this layer, where services exist in isolation (atomic) or as composite services. This layer contains the contracts (service descriptions) that bind the provider and consumer. Services are offered by service providers and are consumed by service consumers (service requestors). Services are accessible independent of implementation and transport. This allows a service to be exposed consistently across multiple customer-facing channels, such as the Web, *Interactive Voice Response* (IVR), or other consumer mechanisms. The transformation of response to HTML (for Web) or Voice XML (for IVR) can be done via *Extensible Stylesheet Language Transformations* (XSLT) functionality supported through *enterprise service bus* (ESB) transformation capability in the Integration Layer.

The Business Process Layer, Layer 4, covers the process representation, composition methods, and building blocks for sequencing process steps. It is through this layer that organizations have another choice for building applications besides custom coding, modifying legacy, or buying applications. Applications can now be constructed from process models using business process management (BPM) technology. Applications can also be assembled using services, BPM technology, custom-coded application parts, and legacy applications.

Data flow and control flow are used to enable interactions between services and business processes. The interaction (for example, submit loan application) may exist within an enterprise (for example, check loan application status) or across multiple enterprises (check credit history using a credit bureau). This layer includes information exchange flow between participants (individual users and business entities), resources, and processes in a variety of forms to achieve the business goal. Most of the exchanged information may also include nonstructured (document images) and nontransactional messages (notify customer of approval). The business logic is used to form service flow as parallel tasks or sequential tasks based on business rules, policies, and other business requirements.

From the interaction perspective, the Business Processes Layer communicates with the Consumers Layer and Presentation Layer to communicate inputs and results with role players (e.g., end users, decision makers, system administrator) through Web portals or business-to-business (B2B) programs. Most of the control flow messages and data flow messages of the business process may be routed and transformed through the Integration Layer. The Data Architecture Layer most often defines the structure of the messages. The key performance indicators (KPIs) for each task or process could be defined in Quality of Service (QoS) and Business Performances Layer. The Governance Layer guides the design of service aggregations. The services should be represented and described by the Services Layer.

The Consumer Layer, Layer 5, provides the capability to quickly create the front end of the business processes and composite applications to respond to changes in the marketplace. It enables channel-independent access to those business processes supported by various applications and platforms.

The Integration Layer, Layer 6, enables the integration of services through the introduction of a reliable set of capabilities. These can start with modest point-to-point capabilities for tightly coupled endpoint integration and cover the spectrum to a set of much more intelligent routing, protocol mediation, and other transformation mechanisms often described as, but not limited to, an ESB. *Web Service Definition Language* (WSDL) specifies a binding, which implies the location where a service is provided. An ESB, on the other hand, provides a location-independent mechanism for integration. The integration that occurs here is primarily the integration of Layers 2 through 4.

The Quality of Service Layer, Layer 7, provides an SOA with the capabilities required to capture, monitor, log, signal non-compliance (for example, security breach) and realize the technical requirements related to the service qualities (such as throughput) associated with each SOA layer. This layer serves as an observer of the other layers and can emit signals or events when a non-compliance condition is detected or (preferably) when a non-compliance condition is anticipated. Layer 7 establishes technical requirements as a primary feature and concern of SOA and provides a way to ensure that an SOA meets its requirements with respect to reliability, availability, manageability, scalability, and security. It enhances the business value of SOA by enabling businesses to monitor the business processes with respect to the business KPIs that they influence. For example, did the approval on the submit loan application occur within the window of time promised to the customer.

The Data Architecture and Business Intelligence Layer, Layer 8, captures the data structure, XML-based metadata architectures (e.g., XML schema), and business protocols of exchanging business data. Some discovery, data mining, and analytic modeling of data are also covered in this layer.

The Governance Layer, Layer 9, should include an extensible and flexible SOA governance framework that includes QoS and KPIs. This layer is responsible for maintaining the service registry and repository, the definition of rules and policies, and the capability to configure SOA at design time and runtime. For example, rules and policies residing in the Governance Layer can be configured as a switchboard for SOA, allowing throttling and adjustments necessary to balance the conflicting demands for service response time and availability, and to restrict access based on context.

62. How Does SOA Differ from Earlier Approaches, such as DCE or CORBA?

The difference between SOA and earlier approaches, such as *Distributed Computing Environment* (DCE) or *Common Object Request Broken Architecture* (CORBA), has a lot to do with standardization. This was initially brought about through the use of Web services and Web services standards. The *Web Service Description Language* (WSDL), *Simple Object Access Protocol* (SOAP), and other Web services standards enable the industry to converge around a common infrastructure model for runtime. Different vendors would have different implementations, but they would generally conform to the base models. The *Web Services Interoperability Organization* (WS-I) is an example of an effort to pull things together so that different vendor implementations are consistent and compliant to the degree possible. Web services, unlike earlier approaches, built upon existing and deployed infrastructure as it took advantage of the Internet, resulting in less cost for adoption and reduced risk.

Agreed upon versus de facto standards is a huge difference between SOA and earlier approaches. Web services standards have been the genesis of SOA, and Web services are more language independent than object-oriented technology integration approaches, which are often language specific (e.g., Java, C, or Smalltalk). *Extensible Markup Language* (XML) is language neutral and renders naturally into languages of choice: COBOL, C++, Java, or others. XML and Web services standards, such as WSDL, have improved flexibility than approaches such as CORBA or *Remote Procedure Call* (RPC) found in DCE, where changes and additions to the data structures often resulted in breakages of the code that used such structures. In contrast, XML does not use offsets, and it is therefore possible to reorder or add data elements without a break in older versions. Web services also use one type space for interfaces, and that type is XML. The other approaches use one type for databases (e.g., SQL), another for in-flight messages (e.g., *Internet Inter-Orb Protocol*, IIOP), and another *Interface Definition Language* (IDL; e.g., CORBA). One approach versus three creates an easier-to-use developer toolkit and *application programming interface* (API) set, and it makes the code base less brittle and easier to change. Contracts that provide a valid sequence of interaction with a service and policies that govern the nonfunctional characteristics of a service have augmented the notion of the interface found in earlier approaches.

One of the most important advances that SOA provides is that the set of services that are required by organizations and captured in the service portfolio provides a business language between business and IT to discuss fulfillment of business needs. A service portfolio is governed as an enterprise asset and used by business and IT stakeholders. This represents a big change from CORBA and RPC, which are something IT uses. SOA and services provide much more than programmatic notions; they provide services at a granularity that the business understands and can use.

63. How Do Web Services and SOA Differ?

The term *Web services* refers to a set of technologies and associated standards that provide one implementation type of the SOA style. Therefore, Web services can be considered to be one realization of or implementation of SOA. There are other options for realizing an SOA. These include *Representational State Transfer* (REST) and other message-based technologies, as well as implementation using traditional technologies. The choice of the implementation technology often constrains the resulting benefits that are expected from SOA. For example, one may choose to analyze and design SOA solutions, and then implement them using a packaged application. Or, one may choose to realize SOA using traditional custom application development techniques such as Enterprise JavaBeans or .NET applications that do not necessarily leverage Web services technologies. Under these circumstances, the full benefits of SOA with loosely coupled endpoints and the added benefits gained from Web services may be harder to implement. Applying Web services is a best practice.

If technological adoptions, lack of skills, organizational readiness maturity, or other reasons preclude adoption of Web services, it is still possible and advisable to engage in service-oriented modeling, design, and governance. In this manner, you can structure the flexibility capabilities your organization requires while sharing common base services, thereby lowering costs over time. Once a portfolio of services is in place, a combination of strategies could lead to increased business performance. One such strategy is to implement the steps in a business process using the services in your service portfolio and to string the services together using a business process management framework or technology.

64. Is SOA too Complex and Enterprise-Level Only?

SOA provides an approach to manage and reduce complexity within a particular scope: whether it be a specific line of business or across the enterprise. Although there is often a discussion of services being deployed as enterprise services, it simply means that the use of a service can be both vertically shared and horizontally shared. SOA has a learning curve to understand and apply, as do all new and incremental changes to software engineering. SOA is not too complex and offers a superior alternative to current practices for constructing application architectures.

Complexity results from several factors: organic growth, unplanned integration with brittle connections between portions of an application and lack of architectural focus. In the absence of technology to force compliance with architectures application teams rely on inspections and the efforts of people to maintain the principles of defined application architecture. Programmers often copy and paste code rather than reuse object classes when making changes, resulting in duplicated code and an increasing large code base. Applications by design are silo and often integrate using hard-wired and point-to-point connections to other applications. Integration logic, middleware functionality finds its way into the application and gets intermingled with business logic code. Processes are buried within silo applications fragmenting the total process. In other words, today's applications reflect complexity. SOA affords the opportunity to reduce complexity in architecture and the application's code base, making impact analysis faster, which results in fewer defects and produces an application built for change.

SOA enables organizations to move from complexity to simplicity in their application portfolios, from tight coupling to loose coupling. Most application code bases today are tightly coupled; changes to one part of the code have a big impact on code that uses it, and this leads to complexity of systems and expense in maintaining them. Business rules are embedded and sprinkled throughout the application. This legacy approach of embedding business rules within application code makes changing business needs difficult to implement. A significant investment has already been made to produce not only the functions in the monolithic application but also to embed the business rules. These two factors make it extremely difficult to reuse application functions and rules, because they are not initially partitioned or packaged for reuse. This creates a tendency to re-create application functionality and business rules with slight variations over and over again in different projects, causing overall project costs to rise. The alternative is to utilize SOA, creating a service portfolio of capabilities that includes the functions and rules as separate entities, easily accessible to and changeable by the business. This capability can be utilized as a consistent shareable portfolio of functionality used in specific areas or across the enterprise.

The notion of a "service" is equivalent to the notion of "business capabilities." These services are capabilities that are then implemented with standardized interfaces that are independent of the implementation details. The *Web Service Description Language* (WSDL) document for a set of application services describes the names and types of data that need to be passed as inputs to request a particular service. For example, a "get Customer Inventory" function may require a customer number and the details of the response from the service; it may return a customer record. These details would appear to be the same whether the function is implemented in Java, C++, COBOL, or so forth; so the requester of the service does not need to know which language was used, and the request can be written in any required language. This allows services from one platform to be integrated in an application written for another platform. The key to interoperability is the request and response message (e.g., using SOAP messaging where messages are coded in XML).

One key benefit of reducing this complexity is the ability to recombine the building blocks of functionality in terms of services in new and innovative ways that support changing business needs. Another benefit that is gained is increased interoperability; that is, the business capabilities or services can be shared among various platforms, regardless of programming language, operating system, computer type, or other technology concerns. The service portfolio is a set of capabilities represented as services and accessible by all projects types: custom development, packaged application or legacy.

65. How Do Interfaces and Contracts Differ?

The service interface defines the operations, input and output parameters, and the results expected from invoking the operations on the service. The service contract can be thought of as including the service interface but extending it to include the expected interaction sequences with the service interface. The contract might include a reference to a policy that defines the behavior of the service interface under certain constraints of a nonfunctional nature (e.g., limitations on the number of transactions per second or a guaranteed rate of response). Figure 7.2 illustrates the message that there is a separation of the service interface from the service realization. The consumer invokes the service contract and uses the service interface accordingly.

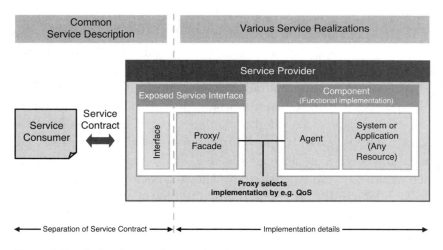

Figure 7.2   Role of a service contract

From a functional perspective, the service contract may define the valid interaction sequences expected of the service. For example, to debit an account, the account must be in an open and current state. It must have enough funds available, and the requester of the debit must have authorization to access the account. To transfer money from one account to the other, a series of interactions is required to call the operations on account service in a certain sequence. For example, transfer funds require a debit. Under the constraint that the account holds sufficient funds, secure transactional context is present, the requesting service consumer has authority to access that account, and the target account is a valid, the initial account is debited, the target account is credited, a message is sent, and the transaction is logged for financial auditing purposes. This sequence of valid interactions is summarized in the service contract. An example of a violation of the contract would be if the operations mentioned are invoked in a different sequence in which prerequisites or preconditions are not satisfied. This would leave the service and its underlying business entities in an inconsistent state. The design of services in SOA should be designed by contract, which is significantly different from designing by interface.

Service interfaces are also different from traditional application programming interfaces (APIs). With service interfaces, there are fewer, coarser-grain interactions; every interaction is the same, and every interaction creates a business outcome. In service interfaces, there is no shared state at a lower level. Contrast this to APIs, which often have many small-grained interactions; often each interaction is different because there is no contract in the design, and frequently there is a shared state in the interactions. Think of the difference between applying for a mortgage over the phone or by mail (i.e., post). A service-like interaction is visible when we use the mail, as the interaction is not dependent on the identity of the service provider. That is, the completed loan application can be returned to a different branch than the one that provided the loan application. Contrast this same interaction when using a phone that is more API like. The interaction is dependent on the specific loan representative—that is, the identity of the service provider.

Figure 7.3 illustrates a service interface and the hiding of the implementation details of the service. Suppliers without knowledge of the details necessary to complete a purchase order request or to cancel an order can use the order service. The order service performs multiple interactions with other services to complete the purchase request.

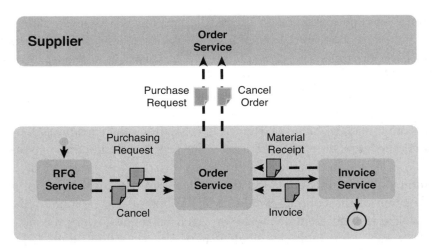

Figure 7.3   Service Interface

Services just specify its own behavior contrasted to a component that specifies both the interface it offers and the interface it requires. Service interfaces are machine-readable and have no identity. Services tend to support "request" based transaction models. The granularity of the service and its interfaces is determined by the usefulness to the consumers and by models of the business.

66. Should Applications Choose WSDL or REST?

Recall that SOA is an architectural style, and that the use of Web services is only one way to implement or realize this architectural style. In fact, there may be a set of different implementations of a service portfolio. Suppose, for instance, that the service portfolio has 100 services; 50 of them may be implemented using Web services, and the rest may be implemented using a combination of *Representation State Transfer* (REST) and *Simple Object Access Protocol* (SOAP). Or, an architectural decision can be made to use other Java or .NET mechanisms that do not use REST or SOAP. SOA does not constrain a solution to using Web services, SOAP, or REST. However, using Web services is a best practice, and using *Web Service Definition Language* (WSDL) is the fundamental aspect of what makes a Web service not SOAP or REST.

Figure 7.4 illustrates patterns. Not all of them promote SOA best practices. Pattern 1 is a tightly coupled interaction, which does not use a Services Layer but may use a service interface in the operational system. In this pattern, it's unlikely that SOAP or REST is used, and most likely a proprietary messaging interface is the transport of choice. In pattern 2, a service component is used with a service interface but no Services Layer is in place. In pattern 3, a Services Layer is present, but the service maintains state in its interactions with the service component and Operational Systems Layer. In pattern 4, a packaged solution provides a service interface and most likely makes REST or SOAP options available. In pattern 5, a business state machine might be in use directly interacting with service interfaces. In pattern 6, a Business Process Layer and Services Layer are leveraged.

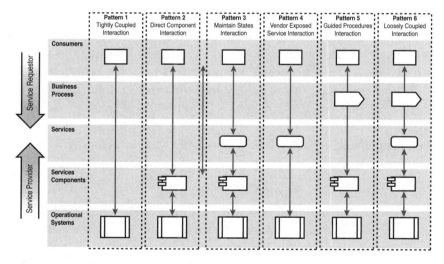

Figure 7.4 • SOA interaction patterns

The primary reason for illustrating the various SOA interaction patterns is to illustrate that there is no right or wrong choice when picking SOAP or REST. Instead, choices may be architecturally weak or strong based on the interaction pattern needed, the quality of service (QoS) attributes that must be achieved, the examination of any constraints imposed by existing operational systems, and the determination of where the greater flexibility lies. One can then make an architectural choice: SOAP, REST, or another interaction. The use of SOAP often is equated as using Web services when in fact Web services can also be REST-based Web services. In SOA adoption, the interaction patterns are architectural decisions along with whether to use SOAP, REST, or other service.

REST is an architectural style that uses the analogy of the state transition diagram and maps that to an application having a set of resources that are connected by state transitions or links. A network of nodes such as the World Wide Web provides an ability to click a link and be transferred to the resource for that link. For example, if you are on a Web page that is a representation of a resource, you are then considered to be in a particular state when you are on that Web page. By clicking a link within that initial Web page that represents the current state, you convey the intent to transition to another Web page, which is really a resource representation of the next state. Thus, a network of states and transitions is traversed by selecting the appropriate link to the appropriate resource. This resource representation puts you, accessing the resource, into a particular state. When you click a link on that page, you get a representation of another resource. When you continue to access various resources by following the links, you keep changing state. This is essentially what is meant by REST.

There are three main differences between Web services and REST:

- **Service oriented versus resource oriented.** With Web services, you are requesting a service (and so this is *service oriented*). With REST, however, you are implying you are looking for a specific type of resource (and so this is considered to be *resource oriented*).

- **Use of HTTP.** REST typically uses HTTP as the transport, whereas SOAP has no restriction on the use of a particular transport. Many people use REST-style interactions using HTTP.

- **Quality of service.** When you use REST, all the QoS parameters must be provided by the transport itself. In Web services, a significant number of specifications must be written to support QoS options, using the WS-*set of standards.

Note that both models have their strong and weak points, and ideally they should become complementary. In fact, the WSDL 2.0 specification provides a harmonization of resource-oriented and service-oriented notions, bringing the simplicity of the REST to the world of Web services implementations of SOA. The motivation behind the WSDL 2.0 HTTP binding is that it allows services to have both SOAP and HTTP bindings. The service implementation deals with processing application data, often represented as an XML element, and the service is agnostic as to whether that data came inside a SOAP envelope, HTTP GET, or HTTP POST. The WSDL 2.0 HTTP binding allows us to expose a service as a resource to be *invoked* using HTTP methods. At the same time, practitioners need to understand that HTTP binding doesn't enable implementation of a full REST-style system. This is still a controversial topic, and will depend on how much value one believes that REST can deliver in a given scenario. The reality is that some scenarios are more amenable to REST implementations than others, which are perhaps more amenable to the more traditional Web services styles of implementations. Having a combination of the best of both worlds is sometimes useful as is portrayed in the WSDL 2.0 specification.

67. What Is the Relationship Between Enterprise Architecture and SOA?

SOA can be applied to different levels of scope: from the enterprise level to individual project level. SOA is integral to successful *enterprise architectures* (EAs), and for some organizations it renews the value of EA. A service portfolio is one of the primary linkages of SOA to EA as enterprise architects play a major role in advancing the use and awareness across the enterprise of the service portfolio. The service portfolio is an enterprise asset, and enterprise architects must play a governance role in the use of services, vertically and horizontally in the enterprise. An architectural review board that includes enterprise architects will govern the service portfolio as an enterprise asset.

The role of EA to SOA is illustrated in Figure 7.5. EA is an architectural discipline that merges strategic business and IT objectives with opportunities for change and governs the resulting change initiatives. SOA represents a strategic business and IT objective that EA helps govern across multiple project instances. EA uses SOA principles and assets (e.g., service portfolio and SOA reference models) to integrate with business architecture, information architecture, application architectures, and infrastructure architectures. EA has an enterprise-wide focus and addresses both SOA and non-SOA aspects of the enterprise.

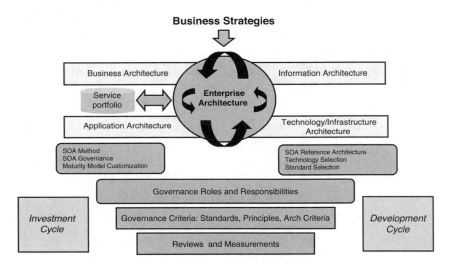

Figure 7.5   SOA and enterprise architecture

EA will use a service portfolio to promote sharing across application silos, across vertical business units, and for the enterprise as a whole. EA has a responsibility for helping with enterprise adoption of SOA; organizational transformation; and enterprise-level communication and visibility for SOA adoption. EA has a primary enterprise responsibility for promoting standardization and governance of shared business and IT building blocks, such as services. Enterprise architects will focus on the following activities related to SOA:

- Incrementally unify software development efforts through a common set of shared services found in the service portfolio.
- Leverage the concepts, principles, and best practices of service orientation at the enterprise level.

- Use the service paradigm to model the common denominator of functionality and map to multiple underlying technologies and development styles.

- Assist with the development of a portfolio of services that have enterprisewide applicability.

- Work with integration centers and applications using a common, shared set of enterprise services.

- Introduce an SOA reference architecture that can be instantiated with various architectural building blocks that can be defined and constrained by the governance applied at the enterprise architecture level.

- Define the reference model for interaction patterns that projects can pick and choose from. These interaction patterns define paths of interaction inside the SOA reference architecture or other architectural standards within the organization, but do not coerce a particular project to be limited to one interaction pattern across the organization.

68. How Do EAI, SOA, and SOI Differ from One Another?

Service-oriented integration (SOI) uses SOA or Web services to integrate applications. It is an evolution from the *enterprise application integration* (EAI), with the additional innovation of using services and service contracts for integration. This enables the creation of a set of loosely coupled interfaces that can interact with one another to achieve the purposes of integration with greater flexibility. SOI is a subset of SOA (although some see SOI and SOA as different, when in fact SOA is broad and accommodates a wide range of adoption scenarios). This range accommodates different levels of maturity, and the range of adoptions produces different business outcomes. That is, some organizations use only SOA centers for integration and don't seek other strategic benefits of SOA. SOI adoption may or may not use an enterprise service bus (ESB) because SOI is simply the adoption and use of services for integration. The utility of distinguishing SOI and SOA is not particularly useful unless SOI is used to describe specific integration patterns or is defined in a manner that provides some unique utility for software engineering.

EAI integrates applications and systems using middleware. EAI solutions are technology based but often not based on standards such as Web services. This is a primary difference between EAI solutions and SOA. Although SOA builds on EAI for integration, it also offers improvements, largely in the use of services. SOA introduces a higher abstraction level than EAI by using services and service contracts. EAI typically uses application programming interfaces (APIs), and SOA uses service interfaces and contracts.

EAI has two main integration patterns: hub and spoke and publish-subscribe. In the hub-and-spoke pattern, an application informs the broker of an event (e.g., a database create, read, update, or delete action performed in the application). The broker takes care of transforming the message, routing the message, and triggering the right action on the client applications. The broker will know, based on internal logic, which client applications to invoke. In the publish-subscribe pattern, the "provider" application publishes events to the middleware, and "client" applications subscribe to these events based on filtering rules. The middleware on a published event will send the transformed message to the subscribing applications.

Another difference between EAI and SOA is that in EAI, often, no direct relation exists between requester and provider applications, whereas in SOA there does. In EAI, applications inform the middleware of some event that took place, but they are ignorant about what happens next. It is the responsibility of the middleware to transform and route the message. In an SOA solution, a client application (the service consumer) calls a service, which is mediated through an ESB, on to the service-providing application. Of course, EAI solutions using messaging middleware could be programmed differently to have such awareness.

69. What Is the Role of Standards in SOA Implementations?

Standards encompass and address infrastructure or communication protocol standards almost exclusively. More recently, standards have attempted to elevate themselves in the software engineering stack. Standards, described as method standards, exist on SOA reference architectures, SOA maturity models, and SOA governance in addition to interoperability or security standards as examples. It is important to distinguish between the infrastructure standards and the software engineering or method-based standards. Method standards represent a new dimension that addresses architecture customization and deployment considerations. SOA is a leading topic due to its newness and the role of services in SOA deployments. Method standards are directed toward IT architects and are oriented toward consistency rather than interoperability or perhaps a different level of interoperability between humans and their designs. Method standards may or may not be best practices, but they provide a level of consistency and predictability.

Organizations should know their infrastructure and method standards. Enterprise architecture (EA) teams benefit from leveraging both method and infrastructure standards. Method standards in areas of reference models and governance models can provide the basis for jump starting a reference model definition in an organization. Method standards in maturity models can help with strategy setting and building roadmaps by EA. Infrastructure standards help define architectural building blocks of an EA.

70. How Should Standards Be Applied to Enable Successful SOA Implementations?

Basic standards are in place for use with implementations of Web services, and these can be used to realize or instantiate an SOA. XML and XML Schema have been standards since 1998 and 2001, respectively. SOAP 1.2 has been a standard since June 2003. UDDI was standardized in the summer of 2003. WS-Security was standardized in April 2004. Well-known standards bodies such as W3C, Oasis, and Open Group have supported the standards. In addition, many "technology proposal specifications" are widely accepted and have been well-supported as "de facto" standards in the interim. For example, until WSDL 2.0 is finished at W3C, the WSDL 1.1 specification is supported by most vendors who claim Web services support their products. The support we have today for Web services standards from major software vendors has led to the widespread implementation of SOA using Web services.

Adopting standards give organizations a greater range of choices when selecting vendor products that adhere to a set of standards. Organizations should select standards to determine applicability and fit to a particular problem. Standards should not be applied without context. Adopting an infrastructure, communications, or software engineering standard should have a defined value and benefit for the organization. Organizations should adopt as many standards as are applicable and for which their appetite can accommodate, as the use of standards helps the future architecture and design of IT systems in areas of interoperability and flexibility.

71. What Are the Common Pitfalls When Adapting an IT Architecture for SOA?

Several common pitfalls occur as organizations seek to apply SOA to their IT architectures. Some pitfalls have to do with governance: organization, business, or application. These concerns have been addressed in previous chapters. The common pitfalls include the following:

- Defining SOA as a new term for *enterprise application integration* (EAI)
- Failure to embed SOA into *enterprise architecture* (EA) thinking
- The lack of guidance or methods on architectural thinking for IT architects
- Poorly defined vision, goals, and measurable metrics for a target architecture applying SOA
- Service proliferation
- Poor adoption and use of reference architecture implementations

EAI and SOA are different, although SOA builds on EAI. SOA is broader than EAI, and failure to focus on its broader capabilities limits organizations to small gains in flexibility because such organizations never exploit the power of services and service orientation in their architectures. SOA must become part of EA because EA is essential to the success of SOA. SOA can be described as the missing link, the link that makes business care about EA as services become business assets, not just IT assets. At the same time, many organizations have no training programs for IT architects. Without the skills of thinking like an architect who cares for the needs of the future, SOA value propositions and how to architecturally realize them never occur in the organization.

SOA requires a meeting of the minds and a shared vision that is published for a future state that embraces SOA. SOA must move from being described in platitudes to being defined with an architectural vision and defined measurements for success.

Service proliferation occurs for a number of reasons and often derails the organizational and business goals around reuse. It also tends to create performance issues, further eroding the organization's confidence in adopting SOA. Adopting guidelines and using governed methods for service development creates a discipline for service creation and avoids proliferation.

Another common pitfall is to ignore the issue of adopting a reference architecture that allows multiple styles of architecture to be implemented including SOA. Many organizations do have reference architectures. Organizations tend to go through phases, having reference architectures emphasized and then deemphasized in terms of priority and importance. Reference architecture should reflect what is operational and working in addition to a future state. Reference architectures should be built both top down as a reference and standard but also bottom up so that deployed and operational infrastructures reflect in the reference architecture. This provides the reference architectural with a pragmatic focus. As part of enterprise architecture and governance, a review of the reference architecture foundations should be conducted. It is also important to adopt and customize reference architectures that resonate with the technical population and are standardized by EA group. These senior architects have their hands on projects and also understand the strategic and holistic vision of the company.

Architecture: Key Concepts

SOA is different from earlier efforts such as DCE and CORBA for a number of reasons, including the arrival of Web services, service contracts, and service interfaces. Although Web services are not equal to SOA, the adoption of Web services is critical to the success of many SOA initiatives. EAI and SOA differ in a number of ways, with differences similar to those between posting a letter (i.e., a service contract) versus talking on the phone (i.e., an application programming interface).

SOA is an approach to architecture that uses services to increase flexibility. Functions are defined and exposed as services. There is only one instance of each service implementation, either at runtime, where each service (e.g., get address) is deployed in one place and only one place and is remotely invoked by anything (mobile device, application, etc.) that needs to use it. Each service is built once, but re-deployed to be invoked semi-locally wherever it is needed. Services enable a common view of heterogeneous systems.

An active and functioning enterprise architecture (EA) group can facilitate the enterprisewide adoption of SOA and keep funding moving forward as results are consistently met. EA and SOA are related, as both need the other. SOA needs EA because of its governance model, its ability to see the organizational horizontally and vertically with new opportunities to use and extend the services portfolio.

8

Information

Information architect: The individual who organizes the patterns in data, making the complex clear; a person who creates the structure or map of information which allows others to find their personal path to knowledge; the emerging 21st century professional occupation addressing the needs of the age focused upon clarity, human understanding and the science of the organization of information.
—Richard Saul Wurman

A significant dichotomy has always existed between the worlds of processing and information and between the dynamic and static aspects of software engineering. Although processing is not fully dynamic and information is not fully static, information pertains to those aspects of the domain that remain constant over time (i.e., the business entities that remain persistent throughout the processing part of an application). Customer information may get updated or transactions posted to an account or ledger, but there is a business entity, account, or customer that is constant. Information plays a central role in information technology. Recall that IT in the past was referred to as data processing because the heart of IT is data and processing of that data.

With the advent of SOA, information is now available as a service. Information is passed to a service through the input message arguments and processed and persisted in the back-end systems. The results are passed back to the service consumer who originally invoked the service operation via a message. Access to a heterogeneous information environment can be sanitized via an information façade that hides the complexity underneath and uses a canonical data model to provide guidance for message schema used by services. Information is a cross-cutting concern that touches the user interface design, workflow, business process design, and the service design. Organizations would like to have information available anyplace at anytime to authorized parties, and SOA enables this goal using information as a service.

In this chapter, we explore questions related to the intersection points between information architecture and SOA. The convergence of information architecture and SOA improves the reuse and flexibility of services. The following questions are asked and answered:

72. What is the relationship between information architecture and SOA?
73. What are information services?
74. How are information services classified?
75. How do information services differ from other services?
76. How should information services be identified?
77. When should information services perform create, read, update, and delete operations?
78. Are information models required for effective SOA implementations?
79. What is a canonical message model?
80. How should a canonical message model be created?
81. Can SOA improve data quality?
82. What are the common pitfalls with information architecture and SOA?

Information: Q&A

72. What Is the Relationship Between Information Architecture and SOA?

Information plays a central role in the message design and flow between services. The information architecture relationship with

SOA is to provide a common structure and meaning for data shared across SOA layers and business domains for all parties in the ecosystem—consumers and providers. It provides a common vocabulary that controls the common definition of terms and facilitates the reuse of services. Without an agreement of terms (e.g., what is a customer, account, address, or name), it is difficult to implement services related to those terms. Both business and IT stakeholders should have a common understanding of business terms, which the information architecture provides. This helps with the proper definitions and corresponding structures to define the inputs and outputs of a service, its messages.

Service messages are more complex than single data types. Messages represent entities and their relationships. Leveraging information architecture data models enhances the design of messages. Aligning the service and data models accelerates design and avoids unnecessary transformations of data between applications or services.

However, this is no guarantee that the quality of the data being returned by services will be accurate. Data, which meets the rules and constraints of its original repository and application, may not satisfy requirements on an enterprise level for a service. Data quality issues might not become apparent within the original application but may cause problems when exposed more broadly on an enterprise level with SOA adoption. Missing values, redundant data types, and inconsistent data formats are often obscured in applications and become problematic when exposed to new consumers in an SOA. The information architecture is necessary for effective and efficient message design of services in SOA adoptions.

73. What Are Information Services?

There is a category of services for which the creation uses information architecture and where a separation of information from applications and processes occurs. This type of service is referred to as an information service. Information services are a specific type of service that encapsulate the underlying information entities and their data sources. Information services can provide processing, consolidation, partitioning, cleansing, validation, and transformations necessary to fulfill a request to access, update, create, search, or validate information or data. Information services consolidate underlying data entities, accessing multiple and disparate information sources, transforming and consolidating the results into a format acceptable to the requesting party, the consumer.

Information services are often used to address the heterogeneous nature of data sources and the fact that data sources often are replicated across several vertical systems. When presented with these two challenges, information services can be used to eliminate inconsistencies in business processes. Reusable, enterprise information can be viewed as sets of business entities standardized for reuse across the enterprise and used to create standard structures, semantics, and service contracts. The goal is to create a set of services that become the authoritative, unique, and consistent way to access the information.

74. How Are Information Services Classified?

Information services allow the consumer to retrieve information in a variety of formats using generic interfaces that increase the reusability of the service across heterogeneous platforms and vertical systems. Accomplishing this goal generally involves classifying information services as follows:

- Integration services that are responsible for data cleansing, data transformations, data consolidation, or federating data across multiple data sources to provide a consistent and authoritative data source. Integration services provide a service consumer access to consistent and integrated data that resides in heterogeneous sources. Integration services are most often read-only.

- Data services handle queries and the typical *create, read, update, and delete* (CRUD) functions. Data services access structured data as a service.

- Content services expose federated content, imaging data, archival records, or record management. Content services manage distributed and heterogeneous unstructured information so that a service consumer can access the content seamlessly.

- Master data services manage and expose trusted master data as services. Master data services provide accurate, consistent, and contextual access to master data from data residing in heterogeneous and inconsistent sources.

- Analytical services provide insights as data is sourced from demographic data stores, merchandise, contacts, transactions from data warehouses, to create analytical information. Analytical services provide access to analytic data out of raw heterogeneous structured and unstructured data. Analytical services are mostly read-only.

Each of these information services can be derived as follows:

- Implementation via a direct access to one or more databases where mapping of the service interface to the physical data schema is the only requirement to identify data elements for input and output messages. However, business rules might exist for addressing the integration of data from multiple data sources.

- Implementation using a preexisting *application program interface* (API) typically used in one or more applications to get at one or more data sources where the data access is only allowed using an application. In this case, the data exposed on the service interface is derived both from the application API wrapper and the underlying data sources. Using only the API may not be optimal because it might not satisfy the needs of the intended consumers of the service, and therefore, analyzing both the API and underlying data to determine the data elements for the service interface yields a more reusable service.

Figure 8.1 illustrates the fact that information services are part of the Services Layer and are access applications, databases, or service components. Like all services described in the Services Layer, the service is realized using components or applications. Information services can be atomic (i.e., single service) or composite services (i.e., aggregates other services) and can leverage multiple applications/databases to achieve their functionality.

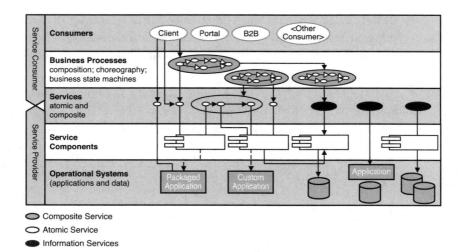

○ Composite Service
○ Atomic Service
● Information Services

Figure 8.1   Information services

75. Do Information Services Differ from Other Services?

Information services are a type of service, and like all services, an
information service can be a reusable unit of business capability or
functionality. With SOA, the word *service* has a specific context; that
is, services are reusable and participate in and are composed in a
value-net, enterprise, or line of business to fulfill business needs.
Understanding the relationship between services and service components can help you understand the relationship between information
services and other services in an SOA.

Services provide the formal contracts between the Consumers
Layer and the Providers Layer. The Services Layer provides the mapping from the business process to the service implementation. The
Services Layer is responsible for identifying the correct service
provider for the request from the consumer, locating the service
implementation, binding to the service implementation, and invoking
the requested service operation.

Service components provide the implementation layer for services. The Services Layer exposes interfaces from the Service Components Layer. There is a many-to-many relationship between service
interfaces and service components. One service component may be

exposed into different formats by different service interfaces. Multiple service components can be combined in the Service Components Layer and exposed in a single service interface. Composite services can be built in the Services Layer to combine multiple existing published services creating a different service. Service components can be clustered into subsystems (e.g., loan processing or order management). Service components can be decomposed further into reusable composite parts comprising the component implementation.

Figure 8.2 highlights the difference between a service style interface versus an API-like style interface. The difference between service interfaces and APIs was described in Chapter 7, "Architecture." Figure 8.2 also illustrates an information service that, in this case, is a request for mortgage information. Unlike other services, information services are focused on returning information that often represents an aggregation of multiple data sources or a snippet of information previously available only in business intelligence (BI) applications. Prior to information services requests for data stored in data warehouses, data marts, or other reporting systems, would require accessing those applications. Now with information services, business intelligence data becomes easily retrieved without the weight of having to use a BI application.

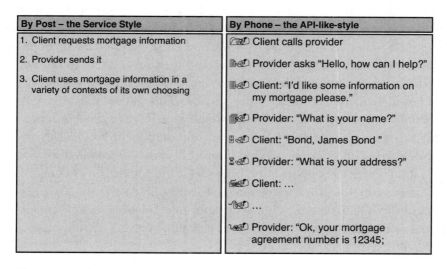

Figure 8.2   Service interface versus API

Service components can be entirely custom coded or service components can be a way of wrapping or connecting to existing components or subsystems in existing operational systems including BI system whether they be Teradata, Cognos, Informatic, SAS, or others. A Service component is an approach for making information services available, as the service component is the connection to existing systems (e.g., BI systems), or it becomes an approach to wrapping legacy systems. In either case, an information service can be exposed.

An information service, based on its functionality, can be the same as a business service. For example, retrieveMortgageData could be a legitimate business service that also happens to be an information service. Information services can be composed in other services. For example, when a business process invokes a service called submit Order, the implementation can be a collaboration between a business service inserting the new order into the Orders system and an information service providing the geospatial analysis data required to allocate order fulfillment to the distribution center nearest the delivery address for the order.

76. How Should Information Services Be Identified?

Chapter 5, "Methods," explored the concept of service identification. There are two primary reasons why practitioners should identify services early in the development cycle instead of making service identification ad hoc—that, is a bi-product of component or object specification. Identifying services early allows for services to be used for structuring the application such that objects and components are identified in the domain of the service. This allows the service to enforce structuring, and it means the service has two aspects: a business area focus and an IT focus later for component boundaries and interface definition. The second reason for early service identification is it increases the opportunity for reuse as the separation of concerns enforced by the service decouples it from other services, making it easier to understand how it can be consumed by processes or applications. For these same reasons, information services should also be identified early in the life cycle.

Answering the following questions can help identify information services:

- Is there a need for data cleansing or data standardization?
- Does the solution require retrieval or maintenance of data without applying any business rules or behavior?
- Is there a requirement to return (read-only) results of a complex data analysis such as hidden patterns, summarization, predictions, relationships, or trends?
- Is there a need for a reusable function to retrieve or update data from one or more data sources for which no existing application exists?
- Is there a requirement to retrieve data from heterogeneous data sources or operational systems?
- Is there a need for data access security so that the existence of an information service allows usage of various SOA security policies to be applied to those services?

Exploring any of these questions and their answers leads to identification of information services. In the same way that not every access to business logic from a consumer goes through a service interface, not every access to data should go through a service interface. Therefore, not every API or every data access should be exposed as a service.

77. When Should Information Services Perform Create, Read, Update, and Delete (CRUD) Operations?

In the early days of SOA, there was a lot of service proliferation, and in some cases information services that were created performed only *create, read, update, and delete* (CRUD) operations. A service should not provide generic access to data such as "give me any information that I need in any format that I define" or simply be a replacement for using a query language like SQL. A query language has greater flexibility for various types of queries and CRUD actions. In most cases, services that are nearly CRUD operations should be augmented by business logic that provides a set of rules for accessing, manipulating, converting, validating, and maintaining the consistency and integrity of the underlying information. CRUD services alone do not provide added value and represent a poor choice of service exposure unless some additional value is provided. There are occasions when information services should be created that largely perform CRUD operations. One example is where fine-grained data access security is a concern, and a separate service allows that security to be more easily performed using security policies. Another, of course, is for any of the reasons cited in the previous question.

78. Are Enterprise Information Models Required for Effective SOA Implementations?

Enterprise information modeling is typically a corporate activity that produces models of the information resources in an enterprise. An enterprise information model is a rationalized set of business entities and attributes that capture the primary abstractions of the business at a conceptual level. It drives the vocabulary and semantics for the enterprise or line of business. Information models by design provide documentation for the concepts being described, and they facilitate the reuse of services and data. So, having enterprise information models makes any architecture that uses such models more effective, including SOA implementations.

In many instances, actual information models exist in silos and in different business units. Different divisions within lines of business may have different information models or data models. Organizations often have many models available, with each describing a portion of the enterprise and each having been developed independently. The quest for a unified and rationalized enterprise-wide information or data model has been one of the holy grails of information architecture. Seldom have organizations been successful at creating enterprisewide information models or data models that are adopted by all lines of business. So many sound reasons exist for creating smaller or line-of-business models as they are easier to construct. In the absence of an enterprise scale data model, models focused on a smaller domain or lines of business models are useful for identifying information services.

Although the physical consolidation and rationalization of an enterprise information model may be an unfeasible endeavor, the creation of a high-level enterprise lexicon of business entities that allows different lines of business to speak abstractly about the fundamental notions of their business is, in fact, a pragmatic and useful practice. Therefore, an enterprise information model can be utilized not for the physical database level of manifestation but for rallying a common understanding of terms across lines of business and divisions within an enterprise. This promotes reuse, which is a key benefit and utility of an enterprise information model. For example, variations of an account entity may have different attributes in different lines of business. However, each line of business can agree on what is meant by an account even though the data attributes may diverge or change over time.

The invocation of a service to process loans, for example, may require a different set of attributes for different business lines (e.g., whether wholesale, retail, or government). However, the fundamental principles of information hiding and process hiding can be applied and combined with information as a service. In this way, a uniform piece of functionality is developed, invoked, governed, and managed across the organization. The underlying implementations will be redirected based on the context in which the invocation is requested. A lookup to a service registry can be made and policies identified and routed to the appropriate service, at run-time, for a given business line. In the same way, the underlying data structures for a particular line of business are discovered through the use of policies and rules. When the context is passed through to a business service for loan processing, it can use information as a service to locate the appropriate information sources to transform and convert data to the suitable format, mapping source to target formats.

Information models and data models are both abstract models, where the information model is not a type of data model, but one that provides representation of business entities their properties, relationships, and operations that can be performed on the entities. This is in contrast to a data model, which describes how data is represented, relationships, and how data is accessed. Service message design benefits from information models and data models. The next answer about canonical models provides a richer explanation about the relationship between these abstract models and SOA.

79. What Is a Canonical Message Model?

The canonical message model is a standardized format in an enterprise or line of business for exchanging information. The model provides the default business data interchange so that services and their components have a standard message format. Of course, all messages passing through the different layers of the architecture might not comply with the model, but rather the model provides the default business data interchange formats so that components need only to know (at most) their own message format and the default message format. The most common representation used for the canonical message model is as a set of XML schemas. This has the benefit of making the type and message definitions directly reusable in the *Web Service Definition Language* (WSDL) schemas that describe the exposed services. A canonical message model consists of the following:

- Defined set of types, elements, and attributes representing the business entities and their business attributes used in all messages. Each definition includes data types, formats, structures, names, and rules governing the allowable values of the type.
- Defined set of messages, each including a related set of the previously defined types, elements, and attributes structured to provide a business document with a specific semantic meaning and context.

A canonical message model should be derived from pertinent information and data models. The canonical data model describes the business entities, attributes, and relationships in a normalized form structured to reflect their business uses. Entities will have connections to other entities based on relationships. Exposure of a service interface must address how these entity relationships are exposed such that sets of required likely reusable information are exposed within the context of the business consumers to avoid proliferation of unnecessary information.

The canonical message model should be designed to support flexibility and extensibility such that the evolving business requirements on the architecture can be easily accommodated. Industry standards and variation analysis can be used to optimize the chosen formats. Implementation through XML schemas provides both the strong data typing rules and flexible structures needed to meet this goal.

Each service exposed in the SOA solution should have input and output messages that are defined directly by the canonical message model or that have a clear and explicit mapping to the canonical message model. This ensures structural and semantic interoperability across all the components participating in the SOA ecosystem.

The canonical message model does not define technical metadata such as routing or security information; it only defines business information. It is common to include technical metadata in the messages passed between systems. Typically, this technical detail can be isolated to message headers so as not to corrupt the business information in the message. Such techniques are common for handling security credentials, transaction states, routing information, message and service versioning, and so on. These metadata can be defined as enterprise messaging standards, but should be kept separate from the business information structures and semantics expressed in the canonical message model.

A canonical message model represents an agreement between different parties in an enterprise or line of business to transform local and often differing implementations or data structures and data sets into a common data format that can be utilized when processing a service. The input format for a message may be in a canonical data format and transformed from an underlying local implementation as the service passes from implementation to implementation, from component to component, which will leverage potentially differing underlying data models. The message format will leverage an underlying canonical message model that is accepted across the transaction path. This is akin to having a business process that cuts across multiple lines of business; as the process invokes services on each line of business, there is a common understanding of the overarching message model.

80. How Should a Canonical Message Model Be Created?

Several objectives for canonical message models influence how they should be created. That is, creating a canonical message model fulfills one or more of these objectives:

- Aligns the information exposed in service messages with defined information models where each message or message element is clearly defined for both structure and semantic meaning within the business context for which it is intended to be used
- Aligns the information exposed in service messages with the accepted business view developed in the logical data model, increasing reuse among service providers and consumers
- Accelerates the development of new messages by providing a standard set of information shared by all messages
- Increases efficiency of integration efforts by providing the default syntax and semantics for information exchange
- Reduces the complexity and frequency that data mapping rules are required to allow different SOA services and components to efficiently communicate
- Accelerates the definition and design of services by providing a set of reusable message constructs from which service interfaces can be composed

The starting point for the canonical message model is defining the data types and complex data types, which comprise the building blocks for messages. Data types can be derived directly from the logical data models. Attributes will map to either XML elements or XML attributes. Entities will map to XML elements. Rules such as value constraints, semantic metadata, and cardinality will also be propagated into the XML schema. The XML schema language cannot completely replicate the structure of a data model in terms of type hierarchies or cardinalities. Each XML message definition is restricted to a tree structure. At the same time, it may be futile to build a single XML message that traverses all the relationships and subtypes of the logical data model, because such a message would be difficult to construct and have no practical usage.

The next step is to identify the candidate message formats. The canonical message model provides a reusable set of types and messages, and defining the messages will require a balance of competing concerns. The resulting message set must be general enough to be reusable. Ideally, each message will be used by more than one service; however, each service must be able to construct messages from the message set that are appropriate for that service's interface. The message format must consider the range of potential message uses in the system along with the most likely areas of extensibility for the messages. Existing application programming interfaces, information models, data models, and the service model are all sources for formulating the candidate message formats.

The final step is to finalize the canonical messages. Using XML or an equivalent is a best practice for the implementation of the message design. Some organizations have created their own version of XML while retaining many of its core properties related to extensibility and flexibility. Using XML, practitioners will make design choices such as how to handle many-to-many and recursive relationships in existing models and other design choices.

Whenever data is shared, either horizontally or vertically, there must be a common understanding between the two participants of both the structure and the meaning of the data being exchanged. If a common data representation is agreed between the participants, such as passing XML messages as defined in the canonical message model, this task is trivial. However, in many cases, conformity to the canonical message model is not possible. For example, legacy applications, legacy databases, packaged applications, and external service providers will all have developed components without knowledge of the canonical message model. Hence, some aspects of the canonical message set may result from data mapping, where mapping occurs from each data format to the canonical message model. During runtime, each participant understands one external data format, which is the canonical message model.

81. Can SOA Improve Data Quality?

SOA is not a silver bullet for improving data quality. However, by understanding the operational data exposed by services, SOA provides an opportunity to leverage services to improve data quality. The level of data quality required to effectively support business operations will vary by applications or lines of business, depending on the data needed to conduct that business unit's operations. For example, financial systems require a high degree of quality data (because of the importance and usage of the data), but a human resources system might have the latitude to operate with a lower level of data quality without significantly impacting business operations.

If data quality issues are present, organizations can pursue preventive data quality approaches that focus on the development of new data sources and integration services or pursue detective data quality approaches that focus on identification and remediation of poor data quality. Data quality detection, correction, prevention, and ongoing monitoring are beyond the scope of most SOA projects, but many of the architecture/application principles related to services can be applied to address data quality.

82. What Are the Common Pitfalls with Information Architecture and SOA?

The most common pitfall is not using information architecture to enhance aspects of SOA solutions. This includes failure to develop or use information models as a basis for message design. It includes not recognizing the need for a canonical message model for message design that is derived from information models. Information models should be leveraged when defining input message formats and output message formats. The service contracts will assume a certain message model that is passed to the service, whether on the input or the output. The *Web Service Definition Language* (WSDL) provides a definition of the service operations, the interface the input and output messages. Information models will facilitate the design of the input and output messages.

Combining information architecture and service-oriented architecture enables both to take advantage of the strengths of each. Information architecture benefits from the use of services, and SOA benefits from having a common understanding of business terms as expressed in information architecture models. Ignoring best practices of master data management, data cleansing, data transformations, and data brokering or information architecture can lead to an infertile SOA adoption where information services are duplicated and no longer can be relied on for their quality.

Another common pitfall is not properly adopting information services as high-value business services versus services that simply retrieve or manipulate data (*create, read, update, and delete* [CRUD] services). Transformation of data from one format to another from one system to another is a key concern of information management. Services can externalize the transformation of formats; not only in the form of the notorious CRUD operations, which create, read, update, and delete information entities, but also to provide referential integrity, consistency, and replication of information and data as needed. Transformation of data from one format to another should be transparent to the consumer of information. Information services do just that—they create transparency for the consumer by shielding the consumer from the complexities of multiple heterogeneous systems and data sources. Information services are responsible for understanding the format in which the consumer needs the information and the consumer does not have to figure out what transformations should be applied to data to obtain clean or quality information.

Improving the effectiveness and efficiency of integration is a goal of many SOA adoptions and one that also requires the use of information architecture in areas of transformation. This represents another common pitfall when organizations don't use aspects of information architecture in this design aspect of the *enterprise service bus* (ESB). The process of transformation often requires an information mediator to access a set of rules and policies pertaining to the access rights, authorizations, and data format needs of the requesting process or service. An information broker or data broker will provide the mediation between the information requester and the information provider as a result of a service invocation.

Information: Key Concepts

Information architecture can leverage and utilize the best practices offered by service orientation to encapsulate information as a service in such a way as to make access to information more loosely coupled, less platform dependent, less implementation dependent, and more consistently available across the organization for wherever the information is to be used.

Creating a canonical message model avoids rework and inconsistent message types, formats, and semantics in message exchanges and integration scenarios. Such models help to avoid the scenarios where each message will be defined strictly within the context and requirements of the message provider and consumer. Such a scenario can lead to proliferation of messages in the solution that offer little potential for reuse and carry a high maintenance cost.

Inconsistent message types, formats, and semantics in systems require that for each new integration scenario there will be a need to analyze the participants and develop message maps to address inconsistencies. The canonical message model plays a role in developing standard, reusable messages.

Brokering data or using services to provide mediation, transformation, and accessibility information to underlying data independent of location to authorized and authenticated users, whether a user interface or an application-to-application scenario, is a cornerstone of information as a service.

Information as a service is more than just a gateway function to underlying data sets. In addition to the transformation and rule application capabilities of an information service, information in the context of SOA may draw upon multiple and disparate and possibly geographically separated data sources. The ability to consolidate information from multiple sources or take a stream of incoming data and break it apart and assign it to multiple target data sources is also a factor of the intersection between SOA and information management.

9

Infrastructure

Infrastructures are flexible and anticipatory. They work with time and are open to change. By specifying what must be fixed and what is subject to change, they can be precise and indeterminate at the same time. They work through management and cultivation, changing slowly to adjust to shifting conditions. They do not progress toward a predetermined state (as with master planning strategies), but are always evolving within a loose envelope of constraints.... Infrastructure creates a directed field, where different architects and designers can contribute, but it sets technical and instrumental limits to their work. Infrastructure itself works strategically, but it encourages tactical improvisation.

—Stan Allen, *INDEX Architecture, A Columbia Book of Architecture*

Comparisons between the construction field and IT abound because of similarities in engineering around infrastructure. Clearly "things"—whether they are applications in IT or houses in construction—serve their end users better when the infrastructure is easy to use. Maintenance of the infrastructure and costs are optimized when the infrastructure is flexible. Architects of infrastructure seek to create flexible and anticipatory infrastructures that meet current and future demands of its end users while at the same time maintaining operational excellence and low cost. SOA infrastructure is not about renovating or replacing existing infrastructure, but about evolving it to address aspects of service orientation, which creates better operational outcomes in business performance. Those outcomes include high availability (so that systems and applications are available when needed) and high performance (so that end users can get their work accomplished when needed).

IT infrastructure is the software and physical hardware used to interconnect users and computers, which includes routers, computers, devices, and a wide range of physical components. *IT infrastructure* is a broad term that encompasses all IT assets, including hardware, software, facilities, and networks. Middleware is often seen as part of the infrastructure, where middleware sits "in the middle" between applications and the infrastructure or between applications and its consumers. This chapter is focused on aspects of infrastructure required for SOA adoption.

Practitioners responsible for development environments, middleware, and the operational environment can benefit from this chapter. In this chapter, we address the various aspects of SOA infrastructure in terms of how SOA addresses flexible and anticipatory IT infrastructures by addressing the following questions:

83. What are the building blocks of an SOA infrastructure?

84. What is an Enterprise Service Bus?

85. What are best practices for creating an SOA infrastructure?

86. What makes an enterprise service bus different from integration technology?

87. How do a registry and ESB relate?

88. How does an SOA infrastructure support events?

89. How should the SOA infrastructure evolve to realize increased loose coupling.

90. How does SOA infrastructure support policy management?

91. How is management of the infrastructure affected by SOA?

92. What is the role of cloud computing in an SOA infrastructure?

93. What are the common pitfalls in creating an SOA infrastructure?

Infrastructure: Q&A

83. *What Are the Building Blocks of an SOA Infrastructure?*

The building blocks of an SOA infrastructure should address the underlying technical infrastructure components needed to support the layers (Consumers; Business Processes; Services; Service Components; Governance; Data Architecture; Quality of Service, Security, Management, Monitoring; and Integration).

In identifying the SOA infrastructure components, Figure 9.1 separates the building blocks into three categories (consumer, functional, and operational) to provide an abstraction that can be used for consistency and reuse across platforms within an organization. That is, engineers (enterprise or infrastructure architects) can use this model as a basis for determining the necessary software products or technologies necessary to provision that building block.

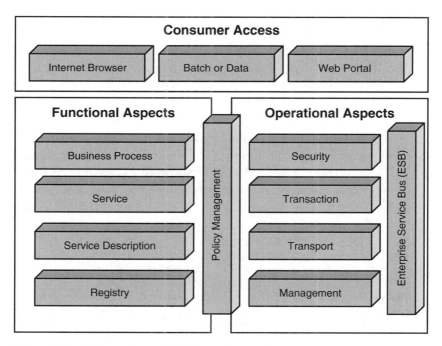

Figure 9.1   Infrastructure SOA building blocks

The consumer access building block includes infrastructure needed to support the various channels for people to access service, including the following:

- Internet browsers where functionality is exposed using a Web interface rendered on a user's browser. Web browsers provide this functionality, and infrastructures today have this component.

- A batch or data channel where consumers can provide or consume large amounts of data. The movement of bulk data over networks addresses raw unstructured data, structured data, images, and any large data that requires high performance. The infrastructure provides a software-based mechanism designed to move large data files using compression, blocking, and buffering methods to optimize transfer times. Infrastructure architectures need to determine whether there are business needs for such a bulk data transfer component and provision accordingly.

- A Web portal that presents information from diverse sources in a unified way. Portals provide an ecosystem of features, which can be achieved using different off-the-shelf technologies.

The functional aspects of the SOA infrastructure are those used by application builders and service consumers to create new business services. These include the following:

- A business process is the building block that supports the development and runtime environment for business processes. Technologies to support this building block include tools for modeling business processes, technology for business process orchestration or choreography,[1] business state machines (also

---

[1] The difference between orchestration and choreography is an active debate. We see both as synonyms for purposes of describing SOA building blocks. Unless there is utility in the distinction, it does not matter for purposes of selecting and provisioning the SOA infrastructure. A distinction can be made that orchestration describes a process flow between services, controlled by a single party; it describes how Web services interact at the message level, including the business logic and execution order of the interactions. Choreography tracks the sequence of messages involving two or more parties, where no one party "owns" the conversation. Most technology make no distinction between orchestration and choreography in their actual realization of feature/functions.

described as process servers), and technology for the automation of workflow, business process simulation, optimization, and management. This building block can help with automation of manual or human tasks and information flow.

- A services building block consists of the application containers (e.g., application servers) and *integrated development environments* (IDEs) that support service design and development. Developers focus on realizing the business logic, assembling and declaring the required quality of service. This building block contains what is often described as SOA middleware and SOA development tools.

- The service description is the building block for creating, editing, and validating service descriptions that are most often *Web Service Definition Language* (WSDL) files. WSDL graphical editors can be used to abstract the complexity of WSDL for developers of services.

- The registry as an SOA infrastructure building block provides a way to define and publish services. Service providers publish, using the registry, the definition of the services they offer using WSDL, any other native service description standards within the organization, and where the service requesters can find information about the services available. The registry is often compared to the Yellow or White Pages of a telephone system.

The operational aspects of the SOA infrastructure illustrated in Figure 9.1 provide for the management and operation of the infrastructure into which services are deployed. These include the following SOA infrastructure building blocks:

- A security building block addresses technology focused on SOA security, addressing Web services security, XML threats, SOA policy management, identity-centric Web services, and security that is focused on authorization, authentication, and identify management. Services rely heavily on the exchange and transportation of data between distributed systems and applications, both within the enterprise and across organizational boundaries to business partners, suppliers, and customers. As a result, an inherent risk exists during the time the data travels between its source and target that it may be intercepted and therefore stolen or modified. This threat is inherently higher in a infrastructure built as a service-oriented environment, where transactions between a service invoker and the service provider are conducted using plain *Extensible Markup Language* (XML) included in a *Simple Object Access Protocol* (SOAP) message, for example. This means that anyone who manages to intercept the transaction can easily read the data included within the SOAP payload. The security building blocks secure the services against these security threats.

- The transaction building block provides for the reliability of a transaction in SOA and a mechanism that ensures all participants in a given environment obtain an agreed upon outcome for a business transaction, financial transaction, or data transaction. These transactions have the following ACID properties:

  - **Atomicity:** If successful, all the operations happen; and if unsuccessful, none of the operations happen.

  - **Consistency:** The service performs valid state transitions at completion.

  - **Isolation:** The effects of the operations are not shared outside the transaction until it completes successfully.

  - **Durability:** Once a transaction successfully completes, the changes survive failure.

  The transaction building block may be provisioned through a variety of means, such as containers (e.g., transaction processing systems or application servers) that provide the ACID properties of a transaction or the infrastructure can prescribe the use of standards (such as WS-Atomic transaction, WS-Coordination, and so on), or the organization can decide that services will be stateless.

- Transport is an SOA infrastructure building block related to the mechanisms used to move service requests from the service consumer to the service provider, and service responses from the service provider to the service consumer. A number of options are available to instantiate components in this building block, and they span from messaging technologies to standard-based technologies that use HTTP, Simple Mail Transfer Protocol (SMTP), or Java Message Service (JMS).

- Management is the SOA infrastructure building block that addresses the monitoring and management of services and the business view or transaction view of their performance. As more and more businesses start to trust key parts of their operations to services, the management of these services becomes increasingly critical. In the case of the SOA, the management building block provides the capability to discover the existence, availability, and health of the services infrastructure, service registries, and service applications. Optimally, the management system should also be able to control and configure the infrastructure and components of the implemented SOA. This includes real-time visibility into process execution such as dashboards, reporting, trending, and alerts. Active intervention as performance data is received is also a part of this component, which may include load balancing, throttling, or bringing new servers online as part of an automated management of the SOA environment.

- Business performance management and business activity management is a part of the operational building block. The management of business services to meet business goals identified as *key performance indicators* (KPI) may require services be instrumented to produce business events that can be used to calculate KPIs and other metrics relevant for the management of the underlying business service.

  Business service policies describe the expected behavior of a business service and eventually define rules dealing with situations where those expectations are not met. The quality of service functions produce IT-level events that report the status of resources used by business services that can be correlated to business events produced by those services. Business- and IT-level events are used by service-level automation to enforce the policies associated with the business services they host. A service bus can be used to collect, aggregate, and evaluate those events for presentation to business process participants in business activity management scenarios.

- The ESB provides a broad set of capabilities dependent on scenarios:

  - **Communications:** Routing, addressing, protocol, publish/subscribe interactions, asynchronous interactions, event handling, and other features

- **Service Interaction:** Interface definition, SOAP, REST, and other features
- **Integration:** Database, legacy, and middleware connectivity; service aggregation, application server connectivity, protocol transformation, and other features
- **Quality of Service:** Transactions and delivery assurance, and other features
- **Security:** Authentication, authorization, non-repudiation, confidentiality, standards support, and other features
- **Service level:** Performance, throughput, availability, scalability, and other features
- **Message Processing:** Message and data transformations, intermediaries, content-based routing, and other features
- **Management and Autonomic:** Service provisioning and registration, logging, metering, monitoring, system management, and other features
- **Appliances:** Parsing, compression, routing, and other features
- **Infrastructure Intelligence:** Business rules, policy-driven behavior, pattern recognition, and other features

Services provide a set of capabilities worth advertising for use by other services; services interact via the ESB, which facilitates mediated interactions between service endpoints. The ESB supports event-based interactions and message exchange for service request handling; in both cases, mediations can be used to facilitate interactions (e.g., to find services providing capabilities a requester is asking for or to take care of mismatches between compatible [capability-wise] requesters and providers).

ESB can be viewed as a set of patterns that can be fulfilled by one or more software technologies, including gateways, and appliances. ESBs can be federated so that to the consumer a collection of ESB technologies operate as a single entity and transparency is achieved with the consumer. Services interact with a single ESB versus having business logic that deals with gateways, different ESBs or appliances as separate pieces of middleware for integration. ESB supports a large number of service interactions in a manageable way.

The functional and operational aspects of the infrastructure SOA building blocks provide for policy management. Policy management is a cross-cutting concern needed by applications at design time and the operational run-time environment.

- Policy management sits in both the functional and operational infrastructure building block classification. Policy management coordinates the authoring, transformation, enforcement, and monitoring of policies across other SOA infrastructure building blocks. Policies can be added to the SOA environment at any stage of SOA adoption. Policies are statements of requirements, and they specify the rules and constraints that govern interactions between service endpoints. Policies can apply to any aspect of the interaction, such as security, mediation, routing, transformations, quality of service attributes, and others. Design-time and runtime policy enforcement are available for SOA infrastructure, where policies can affect developers, business processes, and service interactions.

84. What Is an Enterprise Service Bus?

Enterprise Service Bus (ESB) can be defined in two contexts: design and run-time. As a design-time context, ESB is an architectural pattern that has multiple motivations:

- Supports large numbers of service interactions in a manageable way
- Provides support for advanced service interaction capability, such as transactions, store and forward, infrastructure services, security, quality of service, and so on
- Supports a variety of interaction styles such as synchronous request/response, messaging, publish/subscribe, and events
- Provides a robust, manageable, distributed integration infrastructure consistent with the principles of SOA
- Supports service routing and substitution, protocol transformations, and other message processing
- Supports both Web Services and traditional EAI communication standards and technologies

The ESB pattern can be implemented in one or more of the following hybrids:

- Enterprise Application Integration technology
- Messaging technology
- Technology rebranded or classified as an ESB product
- "Gateway" technology
- Appliance technology
- Bespoke

The ESB mediates characteristics of interactions between service requestors and service providers. The ESB enables the substitution of service providers or implementations transparent to service requesters. The ESB supports a variety of means to attach requesters and providers, and it allows intermediary services to be sequenced between requesters and providers. The ESB may provide a broad set of capabilities dependent on business needs and implementation in several areas, including network communications, integration, security, message processing, quality of service, and service management.

85. What Are Best Practices for Creating the SOA Infrastructure?

Setting up an SOA infrastructure is no different from previous activities of establishing infrastructure for the Internet, e-commerce, or cloud computing. That is, some basic activities should be performed, including infrastructure design, capacity planning, and operability tests to confirm engineered infrastructure operates as expected based on defined and measurable technical requirements.

Best practices include the following:

- Look at the building blocks of an SOA infrastructure (described earlier) and make sure all necessary components have been provisioned. This includes the functional and operational domains.
- Prototype any unknown issues involving performance, availability, scalability, and integration for new SOA technology in the environment.

- Leverage centers of excellence when adopting new technology and when there is a shortage of skills in applications or operations teams.

- Confirm that the schedule is properly resource loaded with people, time, and deliverables to install, configure, and validate all SOA components.

- Make sure that change management procedures work effectively for test and production environments, ensuring that all environments (test and production) have consistent and correct versions of infrastructure software (including middleware, configuration files, and so on).

- Create a production implementation checklist if this is the first time the organization is adopting the platform. For example, this is the organization's first high-volume, UNIX-based system.

SOA adoption tends to highlight any current deficiencies in areas of capacity planning, change management around software versioning, and performance models. That is, if theses activities are ad hoc or not robust, it often leads to breakage and longer deployment cycles for projects adopting new infrastructure building blocks. Performance testing becomes critical for high-volume systems.

86. What Makes an Enterprise Service Bus Different from Integration Technology?

Chapter 7, "Architecture," addressed the differences between *enterprise application integration* (EAI), *service-oriented architecture* (SOA), and *service-oriented integration* (SOI). This question's answer addresses the difference between an *enterprise service bus* (ESB) and integration technology from an infrastructure perspective. An ESB is a connectivity infrastructure for integrating applications and services, in contrast to EAI, which focuses on the integration of applications. ESB infrastructure differs from EAI in the following aspects:

- ESB infrastructure is more than integration because it performs routing of messages between services, converts transport protocols between consumers and providers, transforms message formats between requesters and providers, and distributes business events from disparate sources. Although EAI solutions can address all of these aspects, integration technologies are usually much more narrowly focused. ESB handles a variety of interaction patterns, including events.

- ESB requires management such that the status of a business transaction can be assessed. Has the transaction completed? How long did it take? Did the process step complete? Although the ESB will not be the only technology to assist in business activity management, it will be a part.

- ESB product technologies will be federated such that various technologies (e.g., gateways and appliances) can be used to fulfill a single purpose and provide a single interface to applications. Heterogeneous platforms can be supported allowing different ESB technologies to operate as a single logical ESB.

Figure 9.2 illustrates the reduction of application code that should be realized when adopting an ESB in the infrastructure. EAI infrastructures have matured over the years to assist with the reduction in application code dealing with application integration. Different maturity and adoption levels exist with EAI infrastructures, but when fully realized, EAI infrastructures replace application code dealing with connectivity and mediation but not orchestration or process control. As part of its adoption, the ESB infrastructure eliminates application logic for connectivity, mediation, and process control logic.

Another difference between ESB and EAI infrastructures is the obvious use of services in the ESB; however, the ESB also promotes greater levels of modularity and decoupling of the infrastructure using services. ESBs typically work with Web services and other Internet-based standards, unlike EAI infrastructures. Purpose-built appliances work as part of a federated ESB to enhance performance (e.g., XML parsing of messages). ESBs also use registries to assist with locating services, unlike EAI infrastructures, which often couple the requester and provider.

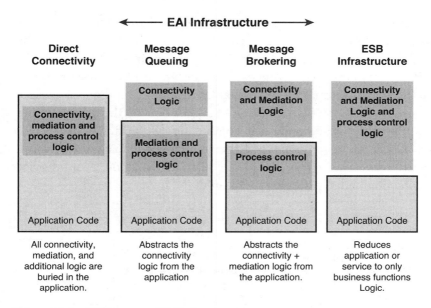

Direct Connectivity	Message Queuing	Message Brokering	ESB Infrastructure

Figure 9.2   ESB versus EAI infrastructure

87. How Does an ESB and Registry Relate?

A service registry supports service life cycle management and governance using an ESB, which is the relationship between the two infrastructure building blocks. Figure 9.3 illustrates the functions of a registry, which includes a repository. A life cycle is illustrated in Figure 9.3 showing five activities/steps. Step 1 is the discovery of existing services that can now be reused and that serve as building blocks for new applications or for use by other services. The ESB can be used to search the registry for such services at runtime or such services can be discovered during design time. But in both cases, the ESB can be used at runtime to locate the service. Newly developed services can also be published to the registry. At Step 2, services can be discovered from other registries or deployed environments.

Change management, versioning, and governance are part of life cycle Step 3, where services are governed using the registry. This ensures changes to the services are authorized and that the integrity of the deployed service is ensured. Consumers of the service can be notified of a change to the service. During runtime is when the ESB and registry have their strongest relationship, as illustrated in Step 4. In Step 5, information that enables dynamic binding of service requesters to service providers is enabled, allowing the infrastructure to enforce registered policies in combination with using ESB and policy management components. Efficiency can be managed by having a registry because it can provide detailed information about service interaction endpoints being monitored.

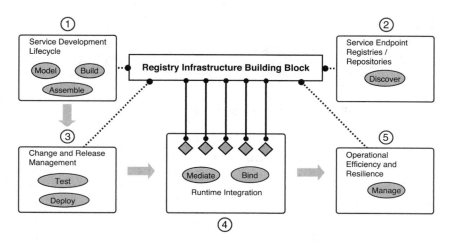

Figure 9.3   Registry life cycle

88. How Does an SOA Infrastructure Support Events?

The ESB can support events and *event-driven architecture* (EDA) in addition to supporting various SOA interaction patterns depicted in Chapter 7. To support events, the ESB should provide EDA run-time features illustrated in Figure 9.4, including the following:

- Storage of events and historical event data
- Event topics that are accompanied with known message models
- Event mediations that provide rules or policies for enrichment, routing, and mediation

- Event endpoint operations to allow the emitting and receiving of events from creators and consumers, respectively

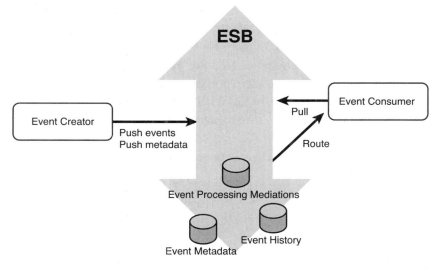

Figure 9.4   ESB support for event-driven architecture

The ESB must provide two-way propagation of event data so that services or applications (both the creators and consumers of events) can operate in real-time notification (push) mode or in retrieve (pull) mode. Services that create events can use data as it becomes available, or the ESB can be enabled to request event data from services on a preestablished time interval using a pull mechanism. This capability enables independence between the mode in which an event message is emitted and the modes in which derived event messages are consumed.

89. How Does the SOA Infrastructure Evolve to Realize the Increased Loose Coupling?

Loose coupling, low coupling, or a decoupled architecture is one of the key architectural principles that indicate a solid architectural design. The design of an infrastructure to support an SOA evolves over time with gradual enhancements. The goal is to provide more decoupling, which enables the infrastructure to change without significantly impacting the applications running on it or, in many cases, the middle-ware that is involved in connecting the applications.

Organizations often start with the need to go from a tighter state of coupling that is more brittle to one that allows for more agility and provides an increased set of capabilities supporting IT and changing business needs. Figure 9.5 illustrates this stage of moving from cou-pled to less coupled. The point-to-point nature of applications can be gradually alleviated by the inclusion of a level of decoupling or indi-rection via an integration layer. Within that integration layer might reside either custom code (discouraged) or an ESB.

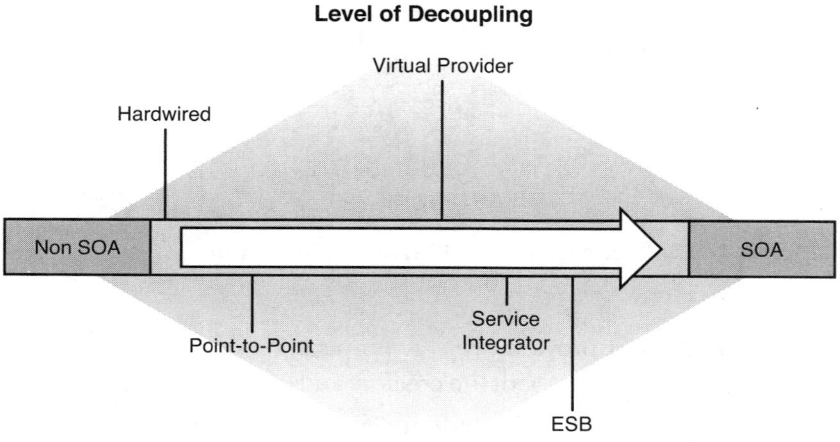

Figure 9.5   Levels of decoupling

In the initial stages, efforts to migrate toward SOA involve a learning and integration curve that organizations must overcome. Figure 9.6 helps pave the way. Practitioners can augment existing infrastructure using this pattern to realize more decoupling. For example, a service provider may access a set of external services, pro-vided by other lines of business or organizations in the ecosystem, without using an ESB. In addition, these services might not meet *quality of service* (QoS) needs in a given snapshot of time required by the service consumer. The virtual provider pattern addresses this issue by allowing a prospective consumer to have less coupling to the provider using the pattern by creating a façade where there is a service interface that isolates the would-be ESB logic or rather separates such logic from the provider business logic. This allows systems or consumers not yet ready to leverage an ESB to make progress. The virtual service provider pattern is, in effect, a place holder in the integration layer, and when this layer matures through the creation of an ESB, the pattern is retired.

Figure 9.6 illustrates three patterns: service adapter, service proxy, and the virtual provider. The service adapter provides a mechanism allowing non-SOA to participate in an SOA ecosystem. The service proxy pattern is where the consumer does not have the capability to directly support services. This pattern allows the use of a service interface by the consumer accessing a service provider. The virtual service provider packages each of these patterns, allowing a migration to an ESB.

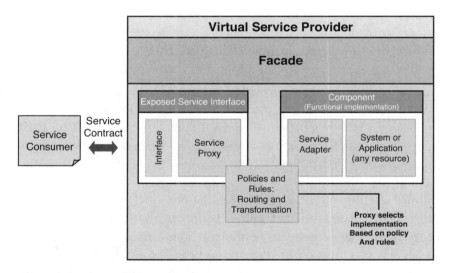

Figure 9.6   Virtual service provider pattern

The service adapter pattern has also been described as a service wrapper. The problem being solved is where legacy systems or packaged applications do not offer well-defined service interfaces necessary for SOA interactions. To provide a wrapper service to a legacy system, some form of adapter technology (or "service adapter") is required. The purpose of this technology is to integrate with the

non-SOA system and apply whatever data or protocol transformations are required to expose a clean service interface representing the
legacy functionality. This interface is published as a "wrapper service." Service consumers can then bind to the wrapper service through
the adapter. The consequence of this pattern is that application or
legacy code can be changed to provide access to a well-defined service interface.

The service proxy pattern solves the problem of where the consumer does not have the ability to access service interfaces directly or
make service invocations using *Web Service Definition Language*
(WSDL). So today, the provider is not providing the functionality as a
Web service but in a legacy format and plans to migrate in the future.
This pattern allows a migration in the future while maintaining service architecture and mitigating changes to the consumer. To shield
the consumer from the sophistication required to access functionality
using a service interface, the proxy pattern operates as a "stepping
stone" providing clients with a service that acts as a surrogate to the
future SOA-enabled capability. This pattern is used in conjunction
with a service adapter for the support of virtual providers.

The virtual service provider pattern is where consumers are
dependent, reliant on a provider for services. Likewise, the provider
relies on the services provided by other service providers. Each
provider wants to operate as a service provider, although *application
programming interfaces* (APIs) are the current mechanism for interaction (i.e., they are not ready to expose services). The service consumer might need to negotiate with the potential providers to obtain
the services required, not only functionally, but with the required
service level agreements or nonfunctional requirements, all based on
a service specification or description provided by the provider. The
virtual service provider uses a proxy to communicate with the legacy
system and an adapter for protocol transformations. The provider
encapsulates the proxy and adapter in a façade because the number
of adapters may increase at random based on new systems and protocols that have to be transformed in the future. So a façade pattern is
used to encapsulate the set of adapters that will allow communication
with existing APIs.

90. How Does SOA Infrastructure Support Policy Management?

With the adoption and acceptance of SOA, new life has been breathed into policy management. The service, service interactions, service composition, and service orchestration are first-class constructs and are baked into development tools, middleware, and infrastructure. As a result, policies can be applied to a service life cycle more than ever before. Policy management technology as a standalone tool and as features integrated into middleware is now available.

Policy management technology allows common policy expressions and semantics for the same policy to be used regardless of specific implementations for multiple services or applications. The recognition of policies by the various SOA infrastructure building blocks (e.g., business process, ESB) permits the enforcement of policies. SOA supports policy management through the service's life cycle, which allows visibility into the service life cycle from cradle to grave.

A policy goes through a life cycle of being created, transformed, or coded to operate in the technology of choice. Enforcement may occur both at design time (e.g., program compilation fails because of policy breach or test cycle surfaces non-compliance to a policy) or run-time where, for example, a security breach is detected where a consumer may not have the authorization to access a service. Monitoring is part of the policy life cycle to verify that the policy behaves as expected with the intended consequences.

Policies can be categorized into one or more of the following:

- Business policies expressed as business statements.
- Business service policies that might prescribe what to do if a service does not meet an expected performance threshold.
- Architecture policies that require the use of a framework or architectural pattern.
- Security policies that might prohibit the use of a service outside of an organization's firewall.
- Design and development policies that prescribe naming standards or adherence to certain measurable artifacts. Enforcement might result in compiler errors when the programmer attempts to compile his source code.

- Operations where guaranteed message delivery is reflected as a reliable message policy. Technical requirements in areas of throughput and availability are examples of operations policies.

Policies need to be defined and enforced, and the policy management life cycle is necessary to properly instantiate enforcement of the policy in its proper tool. Unlike other rules, the capability of a product may affect the type of polices to be defined. We define policies that can be authored and enforced in the chosen technology.

Figure 9.7 illustrates a common problem with policy management. In this example, business policies are fragmented across multiple services/applications and the ESB. Business services with SOA are designed for change, and their policies most likely change, too. If we allow the various technologies that have business policy management capabilities to be the source by which we define policies, we have the problem visible in Figure 9.7.

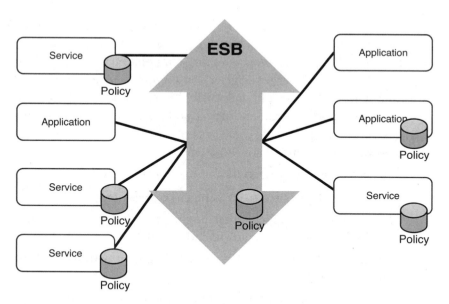

Figure 9.7   Abstracted unconsolidated business policies

Business policies might be defined in a rules engine, application code, the ESB, and other technologies; however, the issue is not an issue of fragmented versus centralized policy management. For example, suppose the business policy is "we want to offer platinum agents a quicker underwriting service that responds within five minutes." The expectation is that the company can determine user context and specify that whenever a platinum agent requests a quote that request will be serviced by the faster underwriter business service. This requires a different architecture for the ESB, as the architecture in Figure 9.7 makes it difficult to change at the policy level. There is no one place to define and reuse a policy that must be enforced across a process involving multiple interactions and services.

Figure 9.8 illustrates an ESB with another function, which orchestrates business policies. It consolidates business-level usage information into one place for easier discovery and change, and behavior can be personalized dynamically based on business context. Policy enforcement and the information needed to evaluate policy are gathered into a single point, the ESB. It therefore becomes much easier, for example, to use business policy to effect dynamic service selection at run-time based on changing business context. This supports greater business agility and responsiveness.

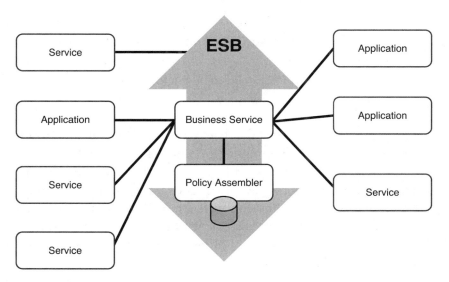

Figure 9.8   Abstracted consolidated business policies

Using business services with policies to dynamically customize the business process based on context (e.g., quote source, delivery channel, location/geography) improves content (e.g., line of business, asset or policyholder, or desired coverage) and contract (e.g., delivery time expectations or appropriate agent credentials in place), providing the flexibility of the infrastructure by having software that provides this policy management capability for business services.

91. How Is Management of the Infrastructure Affected by SOA?

SOA management is the impact to infrastructure as the result of SOA. SOA management is different from prior management constructs primarily because of services. SOA is not only about exposing how you can call a service, but also about defining a set of characteristics for the service interactions:

- How fast should a service respond?
- When will the service be available?
- Who may make various service invocations?
- How many service invocations can be made in a certain period of time?
- What service requests need to be logged?
- How should services be routed?

SOA management lies at the "eye of the storm" created by loosely coupled services. Simply grouping resources by type and managing by silos creates inefficiencies in the process of delivering services and hence requires SOA management. Figure 9.9 illustrates a scenario for SOA management where contracts are established between service providers and requesters, also known as a *service level agreement* (SLA). The focus shifts to monitoring and managing based on the QoS and the service-level objectives

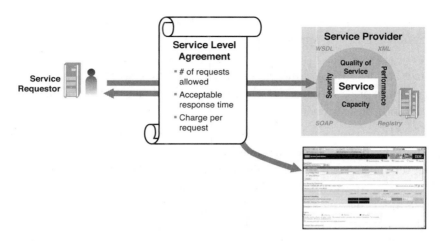

Figure 9.9   SOA management

92. *What Is the Role of Cloud Computing in an SOA Infrastructure?*

Cloud computing is Internet-based computing where resources such as software, storage, services, applications, and development tools are shared. The intersection between cloud computing and SOA lies in what resources that live in a cloud are suitable for sharing in the infrastructure.

A main characteristic of a cloud environment is that it provides elasticity and dynamic capacity on request. Many of the capabilities of a cloud environment are expressed in terms of infrastructure-level services (e.g., platform as a service, infrastructure as a service, application as a service, or even business processes as services). These infrastructure-level services create an optimal deployment environment or operating environment for your infrastructure or subsets of your infrastructure.

Technologies and vendors can be identified who provide an SOA runtime in the cloud. This is augmented with appropriate security restrictions and access restrictions that occurs when multiple organizations run their applications in the same cloud. Some organizations may choose to implement private clouds. Private clouds are often used to describe a cloud environment contained within the firewall of an enterprise, contrasted to a public cloud accessible outside the organizations firewall.

Using the cloud as a run-time environment for SOA is increasingly an option as service-level characteristics such as security and agreements are provided. These will motivate more corporations to consider running parts of their runtime infrastructure in a cloud environment (whether private, public, or a hybrid). Cloud computing is a deployment architecture, whereas SOA is an architectural style. Cloud uses the principles of SOA to build services that will be deployed in the SOA infrastructure. Elasticity is a unique feature of the cloud that can be viewed as the amount of strain the cloud infrastructure can withstand while either expanding or contracting to meet the demands placed on it. These aspects of cloud computing, along with other provided attributes such as partitioning and separation of concerns, are attractive infrastructure features for service consumers and service providers. A key attribute for SOA and its ecosystem is to promote change as business demands changes, and leveraging cloud functionalities may allow organization to change SOA infrastructure faster. Security continues to be the biggest impediment to using cloud services, which is not ameliorated with SOA.

93. What Are the Common Pitfalls in Creating an SOA Infrastructure?

Setting up an SOA infrastructure is no different from the previous activities of establishing infrastructure for the Internet, e-commerce, or cloud computing. However, common pitfalls include the following:

- Lack of a reference architecture to guide infrastructure building blocks
- Exposing existing vulnerabilities in IT processes around availability management, capacity planning, and performance management

- Proliferation of point-to-point infrastructure
- Selecting products in advance of defined business requirements
- Failure to conduct necessary proof of concepts to confirm viability of technology to given scenarios or fulfillment of key nonfunctional requirements
- Propagating ESB infrastructure versus implementing a federated ESB

Reference architectures jump start infrastructure design and are often developed by *enterprise architecture* (EA) teams. In the absence of the EA team having a role in development projects, this artifact is not often created. Teams responsible for infrastructure architecture and design artifact would benefit by having a reference architecture that identifies the universe of building blocks for SOA infrastructure. In this case, the reference architecture can be used as during a mapping exercise to determine what is needed and a plan could be formulated showing how the SOA infrastructure gets built out over time based on project needs.

One key challenge in creating an SOA infrastructure is to come up with the optimal combination of products (often from multiple vendors), which might even include open source, and to integrate these products together. It is important to leverage a reference architecture so that the main architectural building blocks involved in infrastructure are understood and provisioned. The process of checking the relationship between the fundamental architectural building blocks within an SOA infrastructure relies on the relationship between those building blocks (e.g., how an enterprise service bus connects with policy management or the registry and repository or choreography engine).

To choose and procure the right building blocks for the infrastructure, the functionalities and types of architectural building blocks required for the infrastructure need to be identified. This identification and assessment are facilitated through the use of an industry-standard reference architecture such as the one provided by the Open Group or other standard bodies. Teams can utilize the architectural building blocks that are identified as types of components within the reference architecture into layers that pertain to an infrastructure and conduct assessments of whether a particular vendor's products meet nonfunctional requirements and indeed integration requirements with other products that either they possess or that can be procured from other sources. It is also common to leverage open source platforms and products for this purpose.

Organizations that don't perform well in existing IT processes, such as capacity planning, availability management, and performance management, often see breakage when implementing SOA projects. Infrastructure architects should work closely with the application architects to understand the operational needs and QoS attributes for the application to make sure they fulfill these requirements in the build-out of the infrastructure.

Proliferation of point-to-point infrastructures often results from a focus on Web services and the requester/provider interaction pattern where an ESB is not part of the architecture. If an ESB is not being used in the architecture, the application or service should be designed to isolate the connectivity, mediation, and process control from the application. Figure 9.6 illustrates a virtual service provider pattern that can be used to isolate non-business logic that deals with connectivity, mediation, transformations, or any functions properly done in middleware. Figure 9.6 shows the use of a façade by the service consumer that isolates the business logic from coding routing or transformation, and similarly the service adapter isolates the service provider.

Selecting technology products in advance of defined applications that will use the SOA infrastructure often results in products that don't fully satisfy the needs of the applications and consumers of the SOA infrastructure. It's important to have the SOA infrastructure installed, tested, and usable in advance of the applications; however, care should be taken to ensure that sufficient requirements are defined and understood before selecting technologies for the SOA infrastructure.

Choosing the right level of maturity for the SOA target infrastructure ameliorates the risk of selecting technology in advance of defined needs. Although many of the key infrastructural elements of an SOA are well known, not all of them may be suitable for immediate adoption or implementation. Therefore, an assessment of the current and target levels of maturity helps to identify the key architectural building blocks that should initially be used creating a roadmap for the gradual and phased implementation of the infrastructure.

Failure to conduct the necessary proof of concepts is a frequent problem. In some cases, initial prototypes are built that facilitate the selection of a set of products. A lab should be built that tests the integration of the products together, the functioning of the products in an operating environment. This interaction demonstrates the feasibility of integrating the products from multiple vendors and surfaces any issues that occur as a result of utilizing the SOA infrastructure.

The other aspect is the integration of these products with existing applications and with existing operating environment. This latter integration is often overlooked, and it is deemed that the new SOA infrastructure is a stand-alone. This is a common fallacy. The SOA infrastructure itself has to integrate with the existing operating environment, and therefore the touch points of this integration are of primary importance. This is best accomplished with a test.

Regardless of your chosen approach, it is important to conduct end-to-end and integration testing to determine whether the insertion of new SOA infrastructure products negatively impacts nonfunctional requirements in areas of performance, scalability, or availability. It is also important to note that the configuration of the products is of paramount importance.

Propagating or duplicating the ESB is a frequent problem where ESB infrastructure is replicated and exists in silos. This often increases the total cost of ownership and reduces the likelihood of sharing or reusing services in an organization. Federating the ESB allows for multiple products to operate from the consumer vantage point as a single ESB.

Infrastructure: Key Concepts

The SOA infrastructure has basic building blocks that can be grouped into consumer, functional, and operational categories.

The building blocks can be used to identify and build out the SOA infrastructure. The *enterprise service bus* (ESB) is a major piece of the new SOA infrastructure representing a set of patterns and instantiated by vendor's ESB products. The ESB provides matchmaking between service providers and requesters using a registry, where the ESB is an integrated set of tools and middleware services supporting SOA. Cloud technology adds value to SOA infrastructures but presents new issues in areas of security and the type of cloud that should be implemented.

SOA complements event-driven architectures and vice versa, and an ESB should be designed when needed to handle events and an *event-driven architecture* (EDA). A policy manager can be used to add flexibility to an ESB and SOA when dealing with policies and events.

SOA management is a necessity for SOA deployments because the management takes a view of the business process in terms of its performance, availability, and throughput versus looking solely at one service. Application instrumentation may be needed to assist in monitoring coupled with SOA infrastructure building blocks in the form of tools for business activity management and business transaction monitoring.

Several pitfalls are present when implementing the SOA infrastructure. Some notable ones include building out the infrastructure in advance of it being needed and thus causing a mismatch of the required SOA infrastructure with the actual project needs. Failure to accommodate or address SOA governance can create several issues related to successful (or not) adoption of the SOA infrastructure.

A successfully installed SOA infrastructure often matures gradually. SOA infrastructure building blocks are essential for the SOA ecosystem to properly function. The questions and answers in this chapter should help practitioners address core questions about SOA infrastructure.

10

The Future of SOA

The future is not a result of choices among alternative paths offered by the present, but a place that is created—created first in the mind and will, created next in activity. The future is not some place we are going to, but one we are creating. The paths are not to be found, but made, and the activity of making them, changes both the maker and the destination.

—John Schaar, Futurist

Despite the hype and troughs of disillusionment with new paradigm shifts, SOA will remain as an innovation and a set of best practices. This book is an attempt to educate, add value, and expand the view of what SOA is and what it can be. However, what organizations make of SOA ultimately determines its future. This last chapter looks at a few questions whose answers provide insights about the status of SOA adoptions and where is it going. The following questions are addressed:

94. Is SOA dead, stagnant, or moving forward in its adoption?

95. What is the future trajectory of SOA?

96. What are context-aware services?

97. What role does SOA play in embedded or real-time systems?

98. What is the relationship between event-driven architecture and SOA?

99. How does the slow (maturation of standards affect the future of SOA?

100. Do WOA and Web 2.0 affect the future of SOA?

Future: Q&A

94. Is SOA Dead, Stagnant, or Moving Forward in its Adoption?

SOA has reached the "top ten" in effective strategies or visions based on the results of large surveys done by the industry, as recent as 2009. SOA has competed with other strategies: virtualization, business intelligence, standardized application platforms, application harmonization, mobility solutions, and collaboration, to name a few for this distinction. In 2010 and beyond, cloud computing and analytics will move to "top ten" status. The hype around SOA has settled as SOA has entered the mainstream, and at the same time more companies are engaging in earnest with SOA projects.

Companies that have adopted SOA have begun to achieve returns and realize the promised benefits. At the same time, spending surveys show a decrease in SOA spending in 2010 versus earlier years. This suggests that companies are abandoning or stopping SOA adoption plans. So it raises this question: Is SOA stagnant or dead, and have companies ceased SOA adoptions? The answer is the old consultant answer of "it depends," or stated differently, SOA makes sense for some companies but not for all. Of course, even this answer depends on what we mean by SOA, because when we look at the use of Web-based technologies, exposure of services, most if not all companies have achieved benefits representing some level of SOA adoption.

Some company environments and problems present the perfect launching pad for SOA, and for those companies willing to invest, SOA delivers on its promises. Like its predecessor strategies—structured design and analysis, databases, information engineering, object-oriented development, frameworks and patterns—SOA will forever be entrenched as a best practice. Although SOA will not remain as a top ten strategy for transformation or improving effectiveness, it will remain a strategy and best practice for companies looking to improve effectiveness and efficiency. As it matures and becomes part of the landscape, our attention will fade as companies claim and assume that SOA adoption has already occurred in their organization.

In-depth skills in SOA remain scarce, IT departments struggle to mandate strategies as consensus is the norm, and metric thinking and programs are elusive to most organizations, making it even more difficult to legitimize SOA benefits and manage expectations. Current economic conditions make cost cutting and efficiency top of mind, further limiting the number of companies investing, adopting, and moving forward with SOA. However, despite the fact that successful SOA deployment is challenging, large-scale enterprise-scope SOA adoption is underway in every major market where large companies thrive. A significant number of smaller projects are designed to test the waters and gain trust. Plans to expand to other projects and initiatives are underway.

SOA has entered the mainstream and is neither dead nor stagnant as a strategy or approach. It moves forward at the same trajectory and velocity of other mainstream strategies and approaches. New strategies, such as cloud computing, are augmenting the benefits of SOA by, for example, delivering services from the cloud or providing SOA development and operating environments through the cloud. SOA will continue to be the basis of IT transformations until an improved approach for improving efficiency and effectiveness materializes. At that time, SOA will take its place as another building block—another tool that increases the convergence of IT and business.

95. What Is the Future Trajectory of SOA?

The future trajectory of SOA can be seen in several areas. It will be embedded in many of the technologies and paradigms active today and in the future around cloud computing, dynamic business rules management, analytics, business process management, event-driven architectures, and rich user interfaces. The rigidity of package applications, the increasing need for flexible and low-cost integration, the convergence of IT and wireless infrastructures, changing software models and tools, and workload optimized systems will make SOA and the adoption of services a necessity.

A pattern of ultimate ubiquity is evident for all successful IT innovations, and the hype in the marketplace fuels adoption, vendor investment, and company adoption. Early adopters resolve many of the issues involved in the initial implementations, and the technologies and paradigms mature. Systematic techniques, best practices, patterns, tools, and platforms emerge from multiple vendors. As all this progresses, the fundamental constructs of the paradigm change. Ultimately, SOA will be thought of as commonplace and business as usual. This is the greatest achievement of the innovation and paradigm shift after enjoying the spotlight for several years. It merges into the woodwork and becomes part of the everyday work that people do; no longer hyped and yet enjoying a stable and comfortable position among the other paradigm shifts that have taken this path.

Another way of looking at the future trajectory of SOA is to take a look at the Open Group Service Integration Maturity Model (OSIMM) standard. In this maturity model, a spectrum is shown ranging from using services in silo applications to a future of dynamically, reconfigurable services used across an enterprise or with partners. Figure 10.1 illustrates OSIMM, which looks at the enterprise in terms of a set of "dimensions" representing different views (e.g., business and architecture) of the organization's maturity. OSIMM looks beyond any single view of maturity (e.g., process maturity) and examines organization maturity by assessing several views: business, organization, methods, application, architecture, information, and infrastructure.

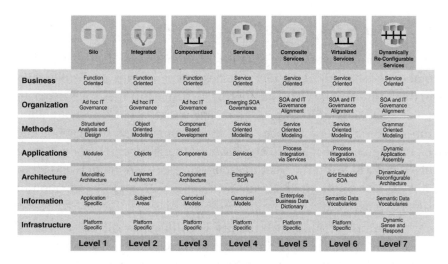

	Silo	Integrated	Componentized	Services	Composite Services	Virtualized Services	Dynamically Re-Configurable Services
Business	Function Oriented	Function Oriented	Function Oriented	Service Oriented	Service Oriented	Service Oriented	Service Oriented
Organization	Ad hoc IT Governance	Ad hoc IT Governance	Ad hoc IT Governance	Emerging SOA Governance	SOA and IT Governance Alignment	SOA and IT Governance Alignment	SOA and IT Governance Alignment
Methods	Structured Analysis and Design	Object Oriented Modeling	Component Based Development	Service Oriented Modeling	Service Oriented Modeling	Service Oriented Modeling	Grammar Oriented Modeling
Applications	Modules	Objects	Components	Services	Process Integration via Services	Process Integration via Services	Dynamic Application Assembly
Architecture	Monolithic Architecture	Layered Architecture	Component Architecture	Emerging SOA	SOA	Grid Enabled SOA	Dynamically Reconfigurable Architecture
Information	Application Specific	Subject Areas	Canonical Models	Canonical Models	Enterprise Business Data Dictionary	Semantic Data Vocabularies	Semantic Data Vocabularies
Infrastructure	Platform Specific	Platform Specific	Platform Specific	Platform Specific	Platform Specific	Platform Specific	Dynamic Sense and Respond
	Level 1	Level 2	Level 3	Level 4	Level 5	Level 6	Level 7

Figure 10.1   Open Group Service Integration Maturity Model (OSIMM)

The business view looks at business architecture and the relation-ship between business and IT. The organization view looks at the maturity of the enterprise and/or business units in the context of organization structure, processes, mechanisms, learning, and gover-nance in support of SOA. The method domain looks at the maturity of the enterprise and/or business units in their use of system develop-ment methods, processes, and related development tooling to sup-port the SOA life cycle. The application domain looks at the maturity of the application portfolio to leverage SOA. It focuses on the use of services for sharing and reuse of business functionality across busi-ness units. The architecture domain looks at the maturity of enter-prise and application architecture to support SOA. The information domain looks at the maturity of the information, data architecture and management to support service orientation. The infrastructure view examines whether the development and operational environ-ment supports SOA.

As this standard emerges and gets adopted, organizations would be able to self-assess themselves not on what others are doing, but on outcomes desired. For example, organizations seeking to take advan-tage of cloud computing for cost containment might look at how they can leverage context services in the cloud. They can examine maturity levels in methods, application, and architecture to see how services are identified, engineered, and deployed. Context-aware services might be the future for a health care provider adopting SOA. For example, such services might offer a chance to improve patient care by sending alerts to patients when its detected that a patient has picked up prescriptions from multiple pharmacies, which if con-sumed in a 24-hour window could have negative consequences. Or for a telecommunication carrier they wish to attract more customers so they offer value added services. One such context-aware service, communicates to a car driver that their present route will not get them to their desired destination in time because of slowed traffic conditions not currently visible and offers an alternative route.

96. *What Are Context-Aware Services?*

Context-aware services provide results or information by detecting cues in the context in which they operate and by responding accordingly. Information needs of consumers are enhanced if the proper context can be recognized. A lot of context-aware examples illustrate the context of location, but context can be abstracted into three categories: human world, physical world, and the business/IT world. The human world context includes personal preferences (e.g., love Indian cuisine), social networks (e.g., proximity to friends), behavior models (e.g., prefer to walk). The physical world context includes geospatial models (e.g., location awareness) and earth-based models (e.g., in the middle of the ocean). The business/IT world context includes business processes or rules (e.g., restaurant can be booked only for parties of four or more), data models, financial models, and decision models. Analyzing and managing these interconnected and interdependent models creates differentiating business value for companies, and it is a direction for SOA, the increasing creation of context-aware services in applications. Services are context aware if they use context (human, physical, or business/IT) to provide pertinent information to the consumer relevant to the task at hand being performed by the consumer.

Smart phones, which often contain GPS technology, provide context-aware services. Using GPS, the location of the handset can be determined as telecommunication carriers make available location services. Applications that use the location service can make available a list of all restaurants or bookstores within three blocks of the location of the device. This exemplifies location awareness, and location awareness in this context is a context-aware service. When armed with location-aware services combined with other services provided by retailers, a new interaction become possible. For example, mobile devices can be used as anonymous traffic probes or as an application that uses the computation power on the wireless edge to reduce backhaul traffic. To estimate the traffic load, the mobile phone acts as a sensor to measure the velocity of movement by using the location of the cell phone, its distance from a cell tower, or the arrival time at cell towers. Suddenly, alerts could appear on electronic road signs accurately estimating your arrival time to a city center.

Mobile devices have increasing amounts of processing horse-power and memory, enabling more and more diverse applications. Just as telecommunication carriers have made available and generated revenue for their business packaging and selling legacy functions (e.g., location awareness) as services, this will become more prevalent as retailers, banks, government, travel, transportation, and other industries leverage their legacy systems to expose services for use and composition on mobile devices. SOA will be the backbone in place for making this more viable for many companies.

97. What Role Does SOA Play in Embedded or Real-Time Systems?

Embedded or real-time systems require a high degree of availability, performance, and response time. Often, embedded systems are responsible for monitoring the health of humans, machines, or services. The role of SOA is akin to its role in providing context-aware services that can be leveraged by embedded or real-time systems. However, the implementation of these systems must address the most stringent performance requirements in latency, availability, and throughout. Therefore, current Web services technologies, for example, might not be suitable for the implementation of such services. There is a class of loosely coupled service implementations that go beyond Web services implementations. They are inspired by SOA service interfaces and loose coupling, and they will be applied to embedded or real-time systems that use mobile robotics and real-time systems that use sensors and actuators within a real-time context.

98. What Is the Relationship Between Event-Driven Architecture and SOA?

Just like SOA, there is no agreement about the relationship between SOA and event-driven architecture (EDA). The various viewpoints see EDA and SOA as competing architectures, mutually exclusive or one as a subset of the other. The primary reasons for these divergent views are a result of the how SOA and EDA are defined. When SOA is defined as Web services or as a request-and-reply pattern or a command-and-control type interaction, it represents a narrow definition of SOA and not the definition provided in Chapter 1, "SOA Basics." Unfortunately, although many people who write about SOA recognize and understand this distinction, many of the blogs and publications on SOA largely discuss Web services and request-and-reply patterns under the guise of SOA.

Figure 10.2 illustrates the two perceptions about an SOA interaction pattern versus an EDA interaction pattern. The perception that SOA prescribes a request-reply synchronous communication pattern is incorrect and is largely due to Web services implementations that use this pattern using SOAP for service-to-service communication. When SOA is described in this fashion, it's largely because there is little to no difference being made between SOA and Web services. The other aspect of Figure 10.2 is the increasing flexibility via loose coupling based on the interaction pattern chosen. SOA supports any of these four interaction patterns, and often the asynchronous patterns are realized using an enterprise service bus (ESB).

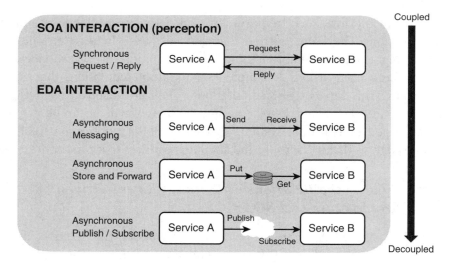

Figure 10.2   SOA and EDA interactions

It could be argued that SOA was inspired by distributed computing and remote procedure calls. However, messaging is a huge part of SOA, and embedded in messaging is the notion of listening for events and responding to events. The Observer design pattern is an example that is utilized in event-driven systems. Once an observer listens for a subject to change, some action needs to be taken. That action can be taken in the form of a loosely coupled service invocation. Thus, the registration of the observers with the subject—that is, the observers or listeners are waiting to observe or listen to events pertaining to the subject—imply that an event in isolation has little value. The registering of an event is not enough. Actions need to be taken based on some policy and a set of rules. The invocation of these rules, the designation of the policies, and the actions that are taken as a result of the designation of the business significant event can be performed through the invocation of services. A policy can be used to select among a set of services available to it the most appropriate service. It then utilizes its rules to invoke the service as an action in response to the condition in which it finds itself.

EDA and SOA are complementary in that SOA allows all the interaction patterns prescribed by EDA and services to be event driven. However, distinct differences exist in the architectural building blocks to support EDA and its interaction patterns. Chapter 9, "Infrastructure," addresses this aspect of EDA and ESB. Optimal SOA implementations do not exclusively apply the request-reply interaction pattern, although there may be instances where this is the optimal architectural decision.

EDA consists of a set of constructs (runtime artifacts, tools, application programming interfaces) intended to support event-driven behavior. Event-driven behavior can be part of a service design where application logic execution is invoked directly or indirectly because an event has occurred. Perhaps one big difference between EDA and SOA is that the various interaction patterns illustrated in Figure 10.1 are designed as services and applications with EDA, whereas with SOA, it's provided externally through the use of ESB, registry patterns, and implementations.

99. How Does the Slow Maturation of Standards Affect the Future of SOA?

Standards adoption and promulgation, and particularly Web services as standards, has been one of the primary drivers of SOA.

Organizations now wonder what impact slow maturation (or even abandonment) of standards will have on SOA. Standards evolve and maturate. This happens independently of the maturity of standards or if a widely adopted standard like Web services or XML should be replaced. Clearly, standards are here to stay. Standards are not settled, but they offer an increased capability for reuse of assets. The mere fact that there are so many evolving standards (more than 100) suggests that the industry is moving forward with adoption of SOA.

Organizations must focus on the standards that matter, the standards that make a difference in their SOA implementations. Standards related to Web Service Definition Language (WSDL) and Extensible Markup Language (XML) continue to be some of the most important sets of standards for achieving SOA benefits. Architectural decisions must be made to determine the context for applying standards where achieving specific quality of service attributes (e.g., latency or availability) will be more important than standards adoption.

The growing maturity and acceptance of the various SOA and Web services standards will make SOA adoptions more standard, increase the number of SOA adoptions, and move the industry in the proper direction. Standards, whether they mature quickly or slowly, will positively affect SOA adoption.

100. Do WOA and Web 2.0 Affect the Future of SOA?

Web-oriented architecture (WOA), like SOA, has varying definitions. Some see WOA as a style of architecture and a substyle of SOA for Web-based applications. Others define WOA as the use of the REST style for building Web services using Web technologies like HTTP and XML documents. Web 2.0 appears to have greater agreement about its definition; and, not as the next version of World Wide Web, but as a platform where software applications are built upon the Web as opposed to upon the desktop. Web 2.0, like WOA, also uses models like REST. Web 2.0 includes mashups and Rich Internet Applications. It's unlikely we will ever see one way to build applications. WOA and Web 2.0 prescribe approaches for building applications, just as SOA.

SOA focuses on a different problem domain than Web 2.0, WOA, or situational applications. SOA has a focus on enterprise applications for many of its value propositions—enterprises where there is a wilderness of heterogeneous systems, a forest of silos, and a vast frontier of proprietary databases and applications. Contrast this to Web-based applications, where standards prevail, hungry consumers are in abundance in the ecosystem, and openness is the law.

Web 2.0 success stories are numerous; after all, designing and implementing Web-based solutions is a lot different from designing enterprise solutions. The widespread adoption of application programming interfaces (APIs), services, and applications from Google, Amazon, eBay, and Twitter make many executives wonder why this cannot be replicated in their enterprise with SOA. This leads to inevitable comparisons of Web 2.0, WOA, and SOA. Executives wonder why they cannot build enterprise applications at the same speed of many Web-based applications. Of course, this is an apples versus oranges comparison. The adoption of SOA is not because organizations want to expose more services, make more APIs available, or offer more interfaces to the Web and its vast consumer base. When the focus is on creating a Web-based ecosystem of consumption, growing, and attracting partners, WOA and Web 2.0 are prudent choices. When the choice is more about making strategic assets of the enterprise more efficient and agile, the problem space changes; SOA is the prudent choice with an adoption that addresses more than service exposure.

Future: Key Concepts

SOA is alive and well, albeit with a fair bit of dissonance regarding its utility. Conflicting reports abound. Some say SOA is not working well in most organizations. Others report that SOA has increased flexibility in all organizations that have pursued its adoption. Some organizations have had false starts with their SOA adoptions; with some abandoning ship and others restarting. Most organizations are adopting SOA, although in many cases, they are targeting specific types of projects, largely integration focused. SOA adoption continues at a steady pace, and more important, SOA has become an engineering best practice often embedded in organizational thinking and methods related to transformation and application development.

WOA, Web 2.0, and event-driven architecture (EDA) are complements to SOA and will remain in the landscape. There are primarily two camps on EDA. One viewpoint specifies EDA as an architectural style in and of itself devoid of any notion of services. Another perspective includes EDA as part of SOA. There are clear differences between EDA and SOA, but the interaction pattern is not one of these differences.

WOA, Web 2.0, EDA, context-aware services, and SOA will remain as implementable architectures and services for the foreseeable future. They will complement each other, as none conflicts with the other. Every approach has its shortfalls, and SOA is no exception. However, the existence of enterprise flexibility and integration problems means that SOA will continue to be the right solution for many organizations for the foreseeable future.

INDEX

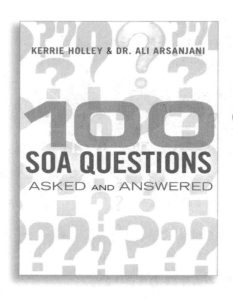

FREE Online Edition

Your purchase of *100 SOA Questions: Asked and Answered* includes access to a free online edition for 45 days through the Safari Books Online subscription service. Nearly every Prentice Hall book is available online through Safari Books Online, along with more than 5,000 other technical books and videos from publishers such as Addison-Wesley Professional, Cisco Press, Exam Cram, IBM Press, O'Reilly, Que, and Sams.

SAFARI BOOKS ONLINE allows you to search for a specific answer, cut and paste code, download chapters, and stay current with emerging technologies.

Activate your FREE Online Edition at www.informit.com/safarifree

> **STEP 1:** Enter the coupon code: QLNEREH.

> **STEP 2:** New Safari users, complete the brief registration form.
> Safari subscribers, just log in.

If you have difficulty registering on Safari or accessing the online edition, please e-mail customer-service@safaribooksonline.com